MW00861125

BUSINESS LAW FOR

ENTREPRENEURS

BUSINESS LAW FOR ENTREPRENEURS

A Legal Guide to Doing Business
in the United States

EKATERINA MOURATOVA, ESQ.

Copyright © 2013 The Law Firm of Ekaterina Mouratova, PLLC

All rights reserved

ISBN: 978-0-9890498-8-7

Disclaimer

The Law Firm of Ekaterina Mouratova, PLLC is pleased to provide this book as an introductory guide for individuals and companies who are just thinking about starting a new business or already have established a venture and desire to educate themselves about the laws and regulations that govern commercial activities.

Ekaterina Mouratova has written this book to assist entrepreneurs and provide them with knowledge and information regarding some of the most important laws and regulations associated with doing business in the United States This book provides a general overview of the legal issues that should be taken into consideration when planning business activities. It covers a broad outline of the subjects that are important to everybody who may be involved in business transactions and operations; however, no part of this book is intended to be an exhaustive discussion of these topics or all possible aspects of the business law. The application of statutes and regulations may vary greatly, depending on the specifics of each particular situation and locality. This book is not an alternative to sound legal advice from a competent attorney relating to the facts and circumstances of each special business need.

This book does not constitute legal advice, and no person should act or refrain from acting on the basis of any information contained herein without first seeking appropriate legal counsel or other professional advice on the particular facts, circumstances, and issues at hand. The Law Firm of Ekaterina Mouratova, PLLC and all contributing authors expressly disclaim all liability to any person with respect to the contents of this book and with respect to any act or failure to act made in reliance upon any whole or partial information contained herein. Transmission of the information in this book does not create or constitute an attorney-client relationship between The Law Firm of Ekaterina Mouratova, PLLC and any reader of such information. Likewise, this book is not intended to serve as advertising or solicitation.

About the Author

Ekaterina Mouratova is the founder of The Law Firm of Ekaterina Mouratova, PLLC. She focuses her practice on business and corporate law, securities regulations, intellectual property, immigration, and real estate transactions. Ekaterina holds law degrees from Pyatigorsk State Technological University (Russia) and Pace University School of Law (New York, USA). With a comprehensive education both in civil and common law systems and a precise understanding of multicultural practices, Ekaterina successfully represents domestic and international clients.

Before becoming an attorney, Ekaterina was personally involved in business. For a number of years, she served as a CEO of the public corporation, a wholesale and retail trade company, with hundreds employees. As a business owner, Ekaterina was drawn to study business and financial law in order to help other business owners develop and grow their ventures and at the same time, protect their rights and interests. Having been on the clients' side of business transactions,, she understands, from a practical perspective, what is essential to accomplish the business purposes of her clients while avoiding the obstacles.

Ekaterina represents individuals and companies in a broad range of industries, including sales, services, manufacture, e-commerce, financial, entertainment and many others. She provides sophisticated assistance and advice to clients in all aspects of their business and legal climates, including organizational, managerial, contractual, employment, and regulatory issues.

Passionate about the law and very dedicated to her profession, Ekaterina is a frequent speaker at seminars and author of multiple publications on business law. She is an active member of the New York State Bar Association, the American Bar Association, and a pro bono attorney via the Neighborhood Entrepreneur Law Project of the New York City Bar Association, a professional community that provides low- and middle-income entrepreneurs with legal services in all business matters.

Ekaterina can be contacted via

email: ekaterina@mouratovalawfirm.com

tel.: (212) 203-2406

Skype: ekaterina.mouratova

About The Law Firm of Ekaterina Mouratova, PLLC

The Law Firm of Ekaterina Mouratova, PLLC, headquartered in New York City, USA, is a national and international firm that provides assistance in the following areas:

- Business and Corporate

- Intellectual Property

- Real Estate

- Immigration

- International Law

The Firm represents individuals and business entities throughout the United States and abroad. It has resources to handle even the most complex matters and render sophisticated solutions.

The Law Firm of Ekaterina Mouratova, PLLC provides all-inclusive services and actively uses its connections with other professionals to accommodate the varied needs of its clients. Whether advising multinational companies on cross-border transactions and joint ventures or assisting individual entrepreneurs with start-up matters, all services are performed in an efficient, result-oriented, expeditious, and personable manner.

The mission of the Firm is to help its clients achieve their goals and succeed, regardless of the circumstances.

The Law Firm of Ekaterina Mouratova, PLLC

154 Grand Street

New York, NY10013

Tel: (212) 203-2406

Fax: (212) 279-9743

Email: info@mouratovalawfirm.com

www.mouratovalawfirm.com

www.law-ny.com

TABLE OF CONTENTS

No one knows what he can do until he tries.

~PUBLILIUS SYRUS

INTRODUCTION

Dear Reader,

Thank you for deciding to acquire more knowledge and information. Life is a succession of lessons, and growth is optional. Winners learn and grow as long as they live.

Most of us assume we are living in the age of free informational flow, but the reality is that truly useful information often comes at a high cost. Even in today's technological age, which makes a plethora of data readily available, reliable and pertinent information is our most valuable resource. We can buy goods and services at any point during our lifetimes, but having the necessary information at the exact moment when it is needed is critical.

If we act with a certain degree of ignorance, there may be no way back to remedy the damage caused by that one misstep. Having the right knowledge at the right time makes all the difference between success and failure. Whether we realize it or not, information is the most important component in all our endeavors.

This is not merely a deep personal belief. As a practicing attorney, I see the proof of the above-stated on a regular basis. Most litigation arises because people did not take preventative measures initially. Entrepreneurs incur great penalties and fines for even minor violations. When I ask people why they did not utilize certain documents and procedures, many of which are very easy to implement, most tell me they were not intentionally trying to avoid legal compliance, but simply were unaware of the requirements.

Unfortunately, business owners and other people spend lots of time and money, only to realize they could have avoided all these pains had they known in advance what was actually needed to accomplish their goals. There are always alternative ways of doing things, but to thoroughly realize all of your options, you must possess complete information about the matter; being in the know will allow you the freedom of choice! Instead of being a prisoner to the situation, you should be a master of your destiny.

Entrepreneurs have two basic concerns: 1) how to start a business on the sound ground; and 2) how to manage and grow the business successfully.

There are also two aspects to business law: 1) how to protect the rights and interests of the companies and their owners; and 2) how to enforce the rights and interests of the market participants, ensuring that businesses will constantly develop without facing unnecessary obstacles that may hinder their success.

Life is unpredictable by its very nature. Nevertheless, the right use of the business law and procedures makes most business transactions and operations predictable. The goal of the U.S. business law is to provide entrepreneurs with:

Certainty: Businesspeople can be certain that if they follow existing rules and procedures, their commercial activities will not be interrupted by unforeseen events. Entrepreneurs can develop their endeavors with security, comfort, and consistency, not fearing what might happen.

Variety: The law affords entrepreneurs extensive flexibility in their business structuring, transactions, and operations in order to encourage business development and obtain maximum benefits from their commercial activities.

Significance: The law equally protects and enforces the rights and interests of market participants, irrespective of their size or position in the market. The law applies in the same ways to a sole proprietor as it does to a big corporation. Accordingly, everybody has equal rights and opportunities.

Growth: Given compliance with existent legal provisions, there are absolutely no unnecessary obstacles to business development and growth in the United States. Moreover, the government provides certain incentives for entrepreneurs to actively engage them in business development. State loans, beneficial tax treatments, and free educational resources are only few examples.

You will save lots of time and money if you take these important first steps: do the necessary research, gather all required data, ensure that all necessary documents exist and are up to date, implement certain procedures and install a number of checks and balances. There are many practical, time- and cost-effective ways to establish a stable, well-functioning business entity. Once you create a strong legal and management structure for your business, you can concentrate on business development, participation in various business opportunities, creation of new projects and techniques, and in general harbor a peace of mind, knowing that your business will not be interrupted by some causalties. You should not have to deal with the same or similar issues several times during the life cycle of your business. You should not incur unpredictable expenses, both financial and time-wise. If a new matter emerges during your commercial activities, which you have not dealt with before, you should not have to act blindly and hope luck is on your side. You should know exactly where to look for the relevant information and help.

Do you presently feel confident about the degree of your business and legal knowledge? Have you ever felt that you simply had bad luck with a particular business transaction? Have you felt that others have taken advantage of you or that you've missed some opportunity because of unpreparedness? Have you ever struggled through a problem, only to discover later that you were on the wrong track all along? Have you ever achieved something with great pains, only to realize there was a much easier, quicker way to accomplish the same? Have you been a witness to someone else's professional success and questioned why everything went so smoothly for him or her? Do you feel smarter or more skilled than others, yet you have no idea where to begin or how to manage your enterprise with guaranteed consistency? Have you ever felt as if you're missing some vital information but have no idea where to find it? Have you ever hoped everything would turn out fine, secretly harboring low expectations? Have you ever felt uncertain in your business deals? Have you ever sensed a nagging apprehension about your business activities, even without apparent reason, as if you weren not sure you were doing the right thing? I could go on and on with these types of questions for several pages. There are a great multitude of business practices and industries, and each has its own aspects. Nevertheless, business owners across the board have similar concerns.

Before becoming an attorney, I was a business owner myself, a CEO of a public corporation engaged in wholesale and retail business. Now I represent entrepreneurs and companies of all sizes in various business matters. Having a comprehensive legal education and experience, I often look back at my early years of business activities and ponder my own behavior, as well as that of my partners; I am utterly amazed at how much effort we poured into situations we encountered just because of our own ignorance. Why was the necessary information not available to us when we most needed it? Even that my company was very successful, employing hundreds of employees and operating on a national scale, but how much more could we have achieved if we had not spent so much of our valuable resources on legal matters? I realized even then that the law was involved in daily operations of our company, whether we wanted that to be the case or not. The wisest and most successful man I've ever met once told to me, "If you know the law, you can work in any kind of business," and knowing what I know now, I'd have to agree with him.

Due to my personal entrepreneurial experience, I was drawn to study business and financial law. It became a passion of mine almost immediately. I saw the degree of protection it can provide and the opportunities it can open up for businesspeople. We do not have to hope for good luck; we can plan on it! My purpose in life has become to help other businesspeople to develop their ventures, protect their rights and interests, and avoid missteps along the way. Some may argue that it is impossible to ensure that we will never face any challenges. This is true, but it is possible to eliminate a high percentage of risk with the right guidance and planning. And if it is possible to diminish those risks, why not do it? If something bad happens, is it not better to feel that you did everything possible to avoid it rather than carelessly and blindly stepping into it?

During a course of years I have been representing entrepreneurs and companies in a broad range of industries. I am proud to be able to to make tangible contributions into their success and growth. I am happy to be in the position to meet so many amazing, smart, creative, respectable people and work with them toward the accomplishment of mutual goals. I am grateful to my clients for the wonderful experiences we have shared together. I believe every aspect of our work was meaningful and significant.

Now, I want to give the benefit of a legal consultation to a wider audience than any particular client who requests it. I wrote this book to provide support and guidance to the starting entrepreneurs, as well as to the owners of established companies. Many legalities apply to businesses, regardless of industry or size. Sometimes people are unable to obtain necessary information for a variety of reasons. Accordingly, they just hope for the best without seeking advanced guidance; however, I am a strong believer that no one's development or productivity should be stifled by easily avoidable obstacles. People should have an opportunity to share their work with the society. The success of one person will undoubtedly contribute to the success of many others. As entrepreneurs put lots of time, effort, finances, and heart into the development of their projects, they should be certain that their rights and interests are protected and that they take full advantage of all available opportunities.

The objective of most business owners is to maintain constant professional growth while protecting their endeavors. As business activities may change over time, applicable laws and regulations may also change. In today's world everything happens much more quickly than it used to be. Change is constant in our professional and personal lives. It can be difficult to conduct business in a competitive market without being familiar with new practices and technologies. The business world and the law accompany each other. With development of one, develops another. The time where people conducted business the same way as their predecessors and were happy to rely on practices established long ago by somebody else is gone. Today, new methods, operations, and markets are constantly emerging and opening up. Entirely new industries are created. And, amidst all of this, business practices and legal regulations change accordingly. No matter your role in the marketplace, you cannot be as successful as you deserve if you are ignorant of these. Some procedures are desirable, and others are required. Implementation of the desirable procedures opens new opportunities, while noncompliance with the required ones may lead to serious consequences. Nowadays, lack of knowledge is not an excuse. To be successful, you must not only possess certain informational resources, but you must be able to obtain them in timely. To make a choice, you must have a choice. To have a choice, you must have complete and accurate information.

This book is one of the mail resources that can be used by any entrepreneur regardless of experience, industry, or size of the business. It should serve as a quick reference for various business situations. The chapters herein each deal with a particular aspect of business law, starting with the establishment of a new business entity and proceeding to dealing with various business transactions and operations, employees, regulatory compliance, intellectual property matters, litigation, and many other topics. By covering the issues that may emerge during different stages of business development, this book will provide you with invaluable legal information along the way of your growth. Without a doubt, this will enable you to minimize the risks, take advantage of the opportunities, and fulfill your business goals.

It is important to keep in mind that the law may apply differently in special situations. It is impossible to cover every single possible outcome within only one book. However, the content in this book provides a general overview of the legal aspects that may be involved in the process of doing business in the United States. In addition, you will find guidance in undertaking your own future research if you determine it is necessary in you particular case. For very complex, intricate issues, it is advisable that you seek the help and counsel of experts.

As previously mentioned, this book was written for both aspiring and current entrepreneurs who do not have a formal legal education. It will not bombard you with jargon, legalese, or other complicated citations of the law. It was penned in a very straightforward language understandable to people with or without college degree. For the sake of clarity, bullet point lists, detailed explanations and examples are provided. This book is a working reference source rather than a theoretical composition of the application of U.S. business law. In these pages, you will find useful, practical legal information and advice without spending a lot of your valuable time. After reading it the entrepreneurs will gain knowledge and confidence in their business endeavors. The book will enable you to:

- Better plan the development of your company;

- Be certain about your rights and interests;

- Enjoy better relationships with your employees, business partners, and other market participants;

- Concentrate on your business activities without forced interruptions;

- Save valuable resources for the higher purposes for which they were intended, rather than wasting them on meaningless daily struggles;

• Know what is needed for success;

• Gain a completely new perspective on the business and legal world.

And in the end, I sincerely hope you will be able to share your positive experiences with others!

CHAPTER 1

Establishing a New Business Available Forms of Business Entities

The law gives certain flexibility to entrepreneurs in the structuring of companies. This choice between several legal forms of entities allows entrepreneurs to expedite the beginning of their commercial activities and obtain maximum productivity. Currently, the following business structures exist: sole proprietorship, general partnership, limited partnership, limited liability company, corporation, and S corporation. The efficiency of any of these structures depends on the nature of the business and the goals of its organizers. In order to determine which type of entity is the best for particular commercial activities, organizers should ask themselves:

1. Will I be the sole owner of the company, or will I enter into partnership relationships with third parties later? How much flexibility do I require in daily operations of the com-

pany? What voting and managerial rights do I want to retain for myself, and what percentage of these can be granted to other partners?

2. Is there a need to protect my personal assets from liability that may be incurred during business operation?

3. Do I need to raise substantial capital through sources other than my close contacts or bank loans?

4. What form of tax and accounting system do I prefer?

Business organizers should carefully compare various legal structures in order to determine which will be most beneficial for their business activities. Below, we will discuss the basic characteristics of each legal form of business enterprise.

Sole Proprietorship

In a sole proprietorship, business activities are not separate from other activities of the entrepreneur. This form is best suited for single-owner business that does not have tax concerns and for which potential product and/or service liabilities are minimal.

Pros:

• The owner (proprietor) has sole control over the business.

• It is simple and inexpensive to create and operate.

• Income, deductions, and expenses are paid by the owner, who reports it on his or her personal income tax return. The company is disregarded as an entity for taxation purposes. Though in New York City and some other municipalities, an unincorporated business tax is imposed.

Cons:

• There is no limit on personal liability for business activities. The creditors can go after the owner's personal assets in order to satisfy debt.

• Access to capital and other business resources is limited by owner's assets or personal ability to get loans.

• Business operations are wholly dependent upon the owner's performance; this is risky, in that illness or other factors may impede the owner from working.

General Partnership

A general partnership is not separate from its owners, and the partners are personally liable for the debts of the business. It is best suited for multiple owners, all of whom will manage the company, and potential product and/or service liabilities are minimal for their type of business.

Pros:

• It is simple and inexpensive to create and operate.

• The company does not pay taxes. Income, deductions, and credits pass through to the partners in the portions set forth in a Partnership Agreement, and they pay applicable taxes. Bear in mind that New York City and some other municipalities impose an unincorporated business tax on partnerships that operate within their borders.

Cons:

• Partners are personally liable for business debts and lawsuits. Most importantly, each partner is also personally liable for the actions of other partners. In other words, if the liable partner does not have enough assets to cover damages, creditors can go after the personal assets of other partners in order to satisfy debt that is incurred during the business activities of their partnership.

• It is difficult to remove and/or change partners without dissolving the partnership unless otherwise specified in a formal agreement. The entire business venture dissolves upon separation of a single partner, unless otherwise initially agreed upon. Therefore, it may be difficult to deal with an uncooperative partner; he or she will have much leverage, knowing that business continuity depends on his or her participation

Limited Partnership

A limited partnership has two or more owners; at least one is a general partner and another is a limited partner. The company exists as a separate legal entity from its owners. It is best suited for two or more owners, when one seeks a passive investment with no interest in day-to-day management of the company.

Pros:

• Partners can claim losses and business expenses as personal tax deductions. The taxes are reported and paid by each partner separately. In New York City and some other municipalities, partnerships are subject to an unincorporated business tax.

• Liability of a limited partner can be limited to the extent of his investment. He or she only stands to lose the amount invested in the company, and personal assets are not vulnerable.

• Limited partners do not participate in company management.

Cons:

• General partners are personally liable for business debts and lawsuits, and this includes the actions of other partners. Creditors can go after personal assets of each general partner.

• It is difficult to remove general partners without dissolving the partnership unless otherwise initially agreed upon and formally documented. Accordingly, partners depend on each other's cooperation.

Limited Liability Company

A limited liability company is a separate legal entity from its owners. It is best suited for single or multiple owners who seek protection from unlimited liability and single-level taxation.

Pros:

• Liability is limited to the extent of owner's investment; personal assets are protected.

• Profits and losses may be allocated differently than owners' contributions, upon agreement between them.

• Capital can be raised through the sale of company interest.

• The entity does not pay taxes separately from its members. The income, deductions, and credits are applied to the members in portions set forth in an LLC Agreement, and they report it on their personal income tax returns; however, members are taxed on allocations, not distributions of the profits, so they will owe taxes even if they decide to reinvest the profits rather than take it for themselves. One exception is the unincorporated business tax imposed by some municipalities (such as New York City) when an LLC has more than one owner.

• LLC owners have a choice regarding taxation; they can choose to be taxed as a corporation if it is more beneficial in their particular situations.

Cons:

• It can be difficult to raise capital. The sale of membership interests in an LLC can create concerns or challenges for investors, as not everyone is interested in becoming an official LLC member.

Corporation

Corporation owners are referred to as shareholders. The corporate entity can have an unlimited number of shareholders; thus, this form is best suited for multiple-owner business seeking both limited liability and established procedures for management and funding.

Pros:

• There is limited owner liability for business debts and lawsuits. Owners may only be personally liable in certain situations when their activities can be proven to be egregious.

• Capital can be raised through the sale of stock rather than through bank assistance or personal loans.

• Lawsuits are brought against the corporation rather than against the owners or managers of the company. The payment for liabilities is limited by the company assets.

• There are tax-deductible fringe benefits, including health insurance and retirement plans.

Cons:

• There are many administrative formalities in managing the company (mandatory regular shareholders and directors meetings, documentation of every major decision and maintenance of records, etc.).

• Shareholders are exposed to double-taxation. When a corporation earns income, it pays taxes on the earnings as an entity. After that, if a corporation distributes dividends to its shareholders, the shareholders are taxed again on that dividend income. Shareholders first pay taxes on the overall profit as a company, then secondarily pay taxes on individual share of profit. Double-taxation may be mitigated by expenses and losses. Also, corporate income may be distributed in form of compensation rather than dividends, but this may be done only to the shareholders, who are simultaneously employees of the company.

S Corporation

Generally, an S corporation is a closely-held company, a good choice for small or family businesses that seek to avoid the double-taxation imposed on a corporate entity, while preserving limited liability and established procedures for business operations and funding.

Pros:

• The S corporation offers all advantages of a regular corporation.

• In addition, there is only one level of taxation. The company does not pay taxes on income, and only shareholders pay taxes. However, shareholders do owe taxes on business income even if the profits are not distributed (for example, reinvested in the business). This taxation form is similar to the taxation of LLC members, except that New York City does not recognize S corporation status for NYC tax purposes, so S corporations in NYC must pay entity-level city taxes if the business is located in New York City.

Cons:

• The company may not have more than 100 shareholders and cannot publicly trade its shares.

• Nonresident aliens (residents of other states) cannot be shareholders.

• Generally, another corporation, an LLC, or a partnership cannot be a shareholder; only individuals can buy shares.

• Administrative duties can be complex for small business owners. They have to go through extensive procedures in order to set up, operate, and dismantle the company.

This overview of various types of legal business enterprise structures should give you an understanding of the pros and cons for each, enabling you to decide what will work best for you and your business practices. To make an optimal decision regarding the form as well as applicable taxation, you should individually consult with a business attorney and discuss all features pertaining to these structures in greater detail.

CHAPTER 2

Buying An Existing U.S. Company

Entrepreneurs may prefer to buy an already existing company instead of starting a new one. This allows them to avoid dealing with star-up matters and to acquire a developed business entity with an existing reputation, connections, contracts, and customer base. The main issue in this situation is the risk of inheriting not only the privileges of that company, but also any drawbacks that may be present. One of the main concerns of the buyer should be present liabilities and the possibility of their emergence in the future. Improper legal compliance, as well as other types of noncompliance, may bring negative consequences long after the transaction is completed.

There are various ways to structure the acquisition of the existing business. The preferred method depends on the present facts, the buyer's and seller's purposes and goals, and the possibility of limiting liability and reducing tax burden. All available methods should be carefully considered and discussed with an attorney as soon as the parties express interest in a deal and certainly before proceeding with further negotiations.

Most acquisitions are accomplished by way of a stock or membership interest purchase, an assets purchase, or a merger. Each has its particular upsides and downsides for the buyer and the seller. You should be aware of these and evaluate each carefully before making a decision to buy.

Stock or Membership Interest Acquisition

The purchase of shares or membership interest may be a simple form of acquisition if there are only a few stock or interest holders and all are willing to sell. However, if it is a publicly traded company with more that 500 shareholders and the buyer is acquiring 5 percent or more of the company's interest, he or she has to provide certain disclosures and register with the Securities and Exchange Commission (SEC), the primary federal agency that regulates securities transactions within the United States. If the buyer is acquiring the interest in the target company not with cash but by exchanging company's securities for the securities of the target company, the buyer also has to file certain information and disclosures with the SEC. One of the SEC's primary functions is to ensure full and accurate disclosure of financial and business information on all securities bought and sold in the United States. The SEC has authority to bring enforcement actions for noncompliance, which may result in extremely high penalties and even criminal charges if some kind of bad intent is detected.

Advantages: When shares are acquired, all assets remain in the target company, including its contracts, intellectual property, licenses, permits, and franchises. Few transfer documents are required. Transfer taxes are relatively low or nonexistent. However, the requirements for special permits and licenses must be verified before the transaction to make sure a change in company control will not automatically terminate the existing ones. The buyer should be certain whether or not he or she will be required to apply for those documents again.

Disadvantages: The main disadvantage in a share or membership interest acquisition is that the target company will usually retain its tax attributes, both favorable and unfavorable. Assuming that the business is continued, all legal liabilities—past, present. and the ones that may appear in the future—are transferred to the new owner. The new owner is fully responsible for all liabilities, taking the place of the previous owner(s). Nevertheless, it is possible to negotiate the allocation of liability between the buyer and the seller in the purchase agreement and have the seller agree to indemnify the buyer in case of undisclosed or unforeseen liabilities. Also, the transaction may be cumbersome if the buyer does not want to acquire a target company in its entirety. If the buyer is not interested in some part of the target company's business field or assets, it is better to consider another method of transaction. In certain cases, the target company may agree to get rid of the unwanted business or assets prior to an acquisition and prepare the company to to the buyer's liking. Bear in mind that the legal and tax aspects of a corporate split are complicated in the United States.

Asset Acquisition

In asset acquisition, the purchaser does not buy the company as a whole, but instead selects only the company assets that are of interest. Generally, the buyer then forms a new company, such as a corporation, LLC, or partnership, and this company will acquire all desirable assets from the target company.

Advantages: The buyer chooses exactly what he or she wants. For instance, if one is interested in only one line of business or one division of a company, an asset purchase is the most straightforward way to accomplish this. The liabilities stay with the target company, since it is only selling its assets, but the company continues its existence with the previous owners. In some cases, however, depending on the nature of the acquired assets the liabilities still may flow to the new owners. For example, property taxes are liens on the acquired real estate, and environmental and pension liabilities may become the responsibility of any subsequent owner under certain circumstances.

Disadvantages: Favorable tax attributes, licenses, permits, and contracts of the target company will not pass to the buyer in an asset acquisition. It is not usually difficult to obtain new consent from public or private parties merely because the owner has changed, but it may be time consuming. Each asset must be separately investigated and evaluated to make sure it is not subject to attachment by creditors of the seller or has other inherent liabilities.

Merger

In a merger, two entities are joined by the operation of law. Normally, one entity disappears and the other continues as the successor to its business. All assets and liabilities become the property of the surviving entity. If the target entity, but not the acquiring entity, is to be the surviving company, this is called a reverse merger. To be effective, merger documents must be filed with the state. The target company members or stockholders may be eliminated by buying out their interest in a target company or by converting their shares into the shares of the buyer or any other company.

Advantages: The transfer of all assets and the exchange of target company shares or membership interest are automatic. No separate transfer documents are required. Normally, the transaction is absolutely tax-free.

Disadvantages: As in a stock or membership interest acquisition, all liabilities of the target company flow to the new owner. Also, a merger with a publicly held corporation may be time consuming because of the need to hold a meeting of the stockholders and to comply with the U.S. proxy rules. If a target company is attractive to other potential bidders, they may use this procedural delay to compete for the target by offering an increased price for the shares or creating other obstacles that will buy them time. It is not an issue if a buyer has a preliminary official agreement from a sufficient number of interest holders, which allows the transaction to proceed. Any remaining or disagreeing stock or membership interest holders can be eliminated through a cash-out merger of the acquisition vehicle with the target company.

Due Diligence: Irrespective of how the transaction is structured, due diligence is a must. This process is conducted by attorneys, accountants, engineers, and other professionals, as necessary. They will thoroughly examine and evaluate all aspects of the target company, both positive and negative, in order to determine whether any hidden liabilities may exist or whether some areas require more careful consideration and should be negotiated specifically before the execution of the transaction. For example, a buyer may require assurance from a seller that certain present contracts of the company will be prolonged in the future if the business of the company heavily depends on them, or perhaps the buyer wants to secure the key employees of the company. All these issues should be carefully negotiated in advance. Due diligence may expose some facts about the target company that cause the buyer to reconsider; he or she may renegotiate certain terms, bargain for a better deal, or decide not to proceed with the transaction at all if the overall state of the company is not what was initially presented and reasonably expected.

Antitrust Law: If the acquisition is fairly sizeable, U.S. antitrust aspects should be evaluated. A notification filing with the U.S. Federal Trade Commission (FTC) and the Department of Justice Antitrust Division may be required prior to consummation of a merger. These federal agencies review potential mergers in order to prevent market concentration in the hands of one or just a few companies that may allow those companies to monopolize the market. It is considered that unreasonable and unnecessary monopolization hurts other market participants, discourages economical competition, and leads to other unethical business behavior.

It is important to remember that preliminary agreements may be enforced in the same way as the final ones. Therefore, parties should not agree to something without first privately consulting with their respective attorneys. An experienced attorney may identify some issues or concerns that entrepreneurs may not initially anticipate, will advise them on the consequences of various offers, will propose the best possible solutions and practical tips for structuring the transaction and accomplishing their goals, and will otherwise guide the parties through the whole process, making sure everything goes smoothly and is completed in due course.

CHAPTER 3

Contracts Most Businesses Must Have

Having all the right kinds of contracts in place ensures that business is conducted smoothly, protects from unexpected liability, prevents misunderstandings and arguments between the parties, and helps business owners avoid protracted and costly litigation. The following are basic agreements that companies most commonly need. Of course this list is not exhaustive, other contracts may be necessary depending on the particular industry, but it is a broad-spectrum look at the contracts and agreements that are used irrespective of the business specifics.

Shareholder Agreement, Membership Agreement, or Partnership Agreement

Depending on the legal structure of the company, the owners should have either a shareholder agreement (corporation), a membership agreement (LLC), or a partnership agreement (partnership). These important agreements serve as guidance for the business relationship between the owners of the company. They set forth the transferability of ownership in the business structure, provide for management and voting rights, distribution of profits and losses, deal with the affairs of the business in general, and help to fill in the blanks on many issues that any business may face during its life cycle or afterward. For example, in order to avoid unpredictable difficulties and business disruption, the partners should negotiate in advance the method of business assets distributions in case one leaves the company by choice, death, or any other situation.

Employment or Independent Contractor Agreement

If a company hires employees or independent contractors, the managers should negotiate the terms of those working relationships in a written contract instead of allowing the general employment laws to fill in the blanks by default. By doing so, the management makes clear to the employee or contractor what is expected, what consequences may be for noncompliance, and what severance options are available. Many companies may require their employees to keep company information confidential, to avoid competing with the company in the same business field during a period of their employment or some time thereafter, to assign to the company all ownership rights for the products, services, and procedures they have created in the course of their employment, as well as to restrain from other actions that may be detrimental to the company's overall wellbeing.

Confidentiality Agreement

This agreement binds parties to keep certain business information obtained during their involvement with the entity as a secret. It prevents former associates from taking advantage of this information after their business relationship with the company comes to an end. Business owners should carefully determine what information is considered confidential and clearly state to all parties what knowledge obtained they may or may not use for their personal benefit or for the benefit of third parties. This agreement should be executed with every person who will have any access to insider information. This would include professional consultants, employees, business partners, vendors, investors, independent contractors, and many others.

Service Agreement and/or Sale Agreement

These agreements are made between the company and its vendors and customers. Such agreements set forth definite terms between the parties, manage expectations and liabilities in case of noncompliance, and very often prevent arguments and protracted litigation. If a company supplies goods or provides services, it helps to have one standard agreement that sets forth all its terms and conditions, with respect to whatever is offered for sale. If such agreement is tendered by one of the company vendors, it is very important that a business lawyer reviews it to avoid double-meanings, ambiguity, or missed terms. The signed contract is binding on the parties, and it is vital to know in advance all rights and responsibilities of each party before making commitments on either side.

Intellectual Property Assignment Agreement

If there is a possibility that someone who works for the company (such as an employee, independent contractor, or business partner) may create something for the company, it is in the company's best interest to make sure that person is required to assign ownership of that intellectual property to the company. The law states that ownership of the work product automatically lies with its creator. A work product can include name of the company, trade dress, logo, design, concept, branding, or anything related to the business. For example, if someone creates a website for the company and does not assign ownership of the intellectual property rights pertaining to the look and content of that website, the web designer can subsequently build the same website for numerous other companies; as an owner of the intellectual property, the designer can unrestrictedly exploit that creation. Business owners expect that everything done for their company belongs to them. In order to duly transfer ownership of those creative works (i.e. intellectual property in the form of copyrights, trademarks, or patents) to the company, a business owner should have all other owners, employees, and independent contractors enter into a formal written agreement stating that those rights will be automatically transferred to the company upon creation of the product.

Terms of Use for the Website

Under certain conditions, puffery or advertisement may become an enforceable contract. Also, a company may be held liable if the words or actions of its employees induce an individual or other entity to act in some way. Therefore, if the company owns and operates a website that describes goods or services, it is very important to post an express disclaimer stating what the company agrees to be responsible for and what it does not. Third parties will rely on information on the company website, and it is important to avoid misleading that may cause them to suffer damages. Disclaimers can contain a large amount of legalese, but they only need to be drafted once and reviewed periodically if the business of the company changes.

CHAPTER 4

Human Resources and Employment Law

Human resources and employment are regulated by both federal and state statutes and regulations. U.S. employment laws cover almost every aspect of the employment relationship, from hiring to firing and beyond. There are rules regarding recruiting, hiring, pay, leaves of absence, safety, taxes, immigration, background checks, testing, employment records retention, workplace posters, employee illnesses, injuries, terminations, and other matters. Below, I review the laws that are applicable to any workplace irrespectively of the industry.

Employment At Will

In the U.S., employment is generally presumed to be at will. This means an employer has the right to discharge an employee at any time for any reason—or even no reason at all. An employee is equally free to resign at any time, with no requirement for an explanation. The existence of a written employment agreement or an employee handbook may limit the application of the at-will principle. Those documents may specify that employment will be for a certain period of time, termination may be for cause only, include an advance notice requirement, and/or other provisions. If an employee files a lawsuit for wrongful discharge, courts will examine these written documents, in conjunction with the conduct of the parties to determine whether the employee reasonably relied on the employer's representation to the contrary. Employers must be careful what they promise to prospective employees in pre-hire negotiations. Employment at will doctrine does not protect employees against claims for unlawful termination based on discrimination, retaliation, or in violation of other public policies (e.g. if an employee is absent from the job due to jury service).

Equal Employment Opportunity

There are federal and state laws in place that expressly pro-hibit employment discrimination based on race, creed, national origin, gender, religion, age, disability, sexual orientation, or marital status. Employers' decisions—not only in relation to hiring and firing employees, but also in relation to promoting, demoting, providing additional training, pay, fringe benefits, job assignments, and increasing or decreasing workload—cannot be based on membership in any of the protected classes. Workplace harassment of the protected class is also illegal. Individual defendants, as well as the organization as a whole, can be held liable for discriminative acts.

Employers are also prohibited from retaliating against employees or applicants who exercise their right to oppose unlawful employment practices or who participate in a discrimination investigation or lawsuit. For example, it would be illegal for an employer to refuse to hire a qualified employee simply because he or she previously filed a claim against another employer or to refuse to promote an employee who testifies in a discrimination lawsuit.

The Family and Medical Leave Act (FMLA) is applicable to the organizations that employ fifty or more people. The Act states that eligible employees are entitled to up to twelve weeks of unpaid leave during any twelve-month period for certain medical and family situations (birth and childcare or adoption, to care for immediate family member who has a serious health condition, or for the employee's own serious health condition). Once the situation no longer exists, the employer must restore the employee to the same or an equivalent position. Under the Act, eligible employees are those who have worked for an employer for a total of 12 months (does not need to be consecutive) and a minimum of 1,250 hours during the previous 12 months. The allowable serious conditions for FMLA are those that would result in incapacity if not timely treated. Common colds, headaches, and routine dental procedures are not considered to be a serious health condition. The employer cannot discriminate against any employee who exercises his right to take leave; however, an employer can terminate that employee regardless of leave status if there is a legitimate, nondiscriminatory reason for termination (e.g. a massive layoff).

Hiring

Under both federal and state law, it is illegal for an employer to publish a job advertisement or use a recruiting practice that shows preference or discourages any member of the protected class from applying. As such, employers must be careful about word choice and language in their job postings. Employers should identify the basic tasks and qualifications needed for the specific advertised position, and there must be a justifiable, nondiscriminatory reason for including each requirement. During the interview process, the employer should concentrate on gathering information, which is necessary to judge prospective employee's professional competence. Some examples of inquiries that may indicate intent to discriminate are childbearing plans, marital status, applicant's national origin, religion, and age.

Employers must complete an Employment Eligibility Verification Form for each employee and examine acceptable forms of documentation supplied by the employee in order to confirm the employee's eligibility to work in the U.S. Since employers cannot discriminate based on nationality, employers should not ask whether an applicant is a U.S. citizen; however, you can (and probably should) ask whether an applicant has a legal right to work in the United States.

Evaluation

Employers should make their expectations clear to employees from the very start of the working relationship. As time progresses, employees should be provided with regular feedback as to their strengths and weaknesses, their successes and shortfalls within the position they hold. Employers should apply the same evaluation factors to all employees in similar positions and keep thorough, accurate records of all facts of discipline and termination. During the evaluation process, employers should specify the particulars of employee's conduct without making generalizations about the employee's personality. Management should make sure each employee signs every performance review. If an employee refuses to sign, managers should document this fact by asking two witnesses to sign off a statement of the employee's refusal. In any case, employers must be consistent in applying review and discipline methods to all employees.

Termination

When evaluating whether or not to terminate an employee, fairness is the most important consideration. Grounds for termination must be objectively provable. Red flags that may indicate improper motives in the discipline process or termination of an employee include: decisions made in the heat of the moment, varying treatment of similar employees, excused by law absence from the workplace (medical leave, for example), complaints made by an employee, and other hidden reasons irrelevant to the employee's professional qualifications.

The Importance of Handbooks

Handbooks should be available to all employees for review. They should clearly state company policies regarding all employment situations (vacations, evaluation, termination, workplace conduct, harassment, timekeeping, and other matters). Well-written, detailed handbooks can be your basis for a strong defense in case of a lawsuit by a disgruntled employee or an administrative complaint. Handbooks should be carefully worded and drafted to avoid unintended obligations on the employer. They must clearly communicate the at-will nature of the employment, stating that neither the handbook nor any other document conveys the employee's right to remain in the employment of the company. A well-structured anti-harassment policy can help employers avoid liability for a hostile work environment claim, as it will show that the employer took measures to prevent illegal conduct in the workplace and that all employees are familiar with the policy. Individuals who violate this policy may be held personally liable, but the company will have a solid, affirmative defense. Handbooks should be synchronized with other personnel policies, offer letters, employment contracts, and various agreements.

Employment Contracts

The importance of properly drafted contracts is paramount. These will help you avoid misunderstandings, pitfalls, potential administrative proceedings, claims, and lawsuits. If an issue arises, the written agreement will provide a strong, affirmative defense. Contracts will protect the rights and interests of both parties (employee and employer, in this case) and clearly state expectations, obligations, and responsibilities of the parties. Employment contracts are drafted according to the preferences of the parties involved and include various clauses depending on what the parties hope to achieve by starting their professional relationship. The most common clauses that an employer may wish to includ in an employment contract are non-disclosure/confidentiality agreement, non-compete agreement, and intellectual property assignment agreement.

Within the realm of work duties, an employee may have access to the company's internal information. The employer is entitled to protect its trade secrets and proprietary business information, and prohibit employees from using or disclosing the company's confidential information during the period of their employment, as well as after its termination.

A non-compete covenant is an agreement by an employee not to compete with his or her employer in certain ways for a period of time after the employment relationship ends. These covenants are strictly construed by the courts and can be enforced only if they are in writing, supported by consideration, reasonable as to the duration of the restriction and the territory, and do not violate any public policies.

Intellectual property assignment agreement is an agreement of the employee stating that everything he or she creates during the course of employment, as pertaining to the company, will become the property of the company.

Employers should require all employees to sign a written agreement before the commencement of employment, and the content of these agreements can be incorporated into an employee handbook by reference.

Minimum Wage

The Fair Labor Standards Act (FLSA) is the primary law that regulates minimum wage, overtime pay, child labor, and working conditions and prohibits salary discrimination based on gender. The FLSA is administered and enforced by the United States Department of Labor. Each state has its own laws similar to the FLSA. Currently, at the time of this publication, pursuant to the federal law the required minimum wage is $7.25 per hour. This amount may be modified in certain states. State laws may not offer lower than the federal minimum wage requirement, but they may increase it within their boarders. There are numerous exemption and exceptions from the FLSA minimum wage and overtime requirements. The most common is the white-collar exemption, which applies to executive and administrative employees, as well as to learned and artistic professionals. Various exceptions also apply to full-time students, employees under the age of twenty, employees who earn tips, and so on.

Fringe Benefits

Fringe benefits typically include healthcare (medical, dental, and vision), pensions, paid vacations and holidays, disability, life insurance, and other benefits. Employers are not required to offer any of these benefits, but they may choose to do so voluntarily as an additional incentive for employees.

Workers' Compensation Insurance

In certain industries, companies are required to purchase workers' compensation insurance. This is typical in industries in which the risk of injury during the job performance is high (construction and manufacturing, for example). Workers' compensation insurance provides compensation for medical care expenses incurred by employees who are injured on the job.

Disability Insurance

Some states require employers to provide partial wage replacement insurance coverage to their eligible employees for non-work-related sickness or injury. Disability benefits include cash payments only. Medical care is the responsibility of the claimant. Employers in certain states (New York, New Jersey, California, Rhode Island, and Hawaii) are required to purchase disability insurance if they have one or more employees. There are a number of exceptions relieving the employers from this obligation.

Payroll and Employment Taxes

Federal and state regulations require employers to withhold and remit income and Social Security taxes to the appropriate government agencies and to file regular payroll tax returns. Federal and state penalties may be assessed for failure to properly withhold tax and report wages paid to employees. Employers may be personally liable for unpaid payroll taxes.

It is much more convenient, time efficient, and preferable from legal perspective to set up personnel systems that comply with applicable federal and state laws, either at the earliest stage of establishing a business entity or before hiring employees. It is more cost effective to implement good practices and forms *before* any issue arises than to deal with law enforcement agencies or complaining parties later.

Employees vs. Independent Contractors

When there is a need for additional help beyond the capabilities or feasible workload of regular employees, often companies face a decision whom better to hire – an employee or an independent contractor. The choice between hiring regular employees or independent contractors may be a difficult one. There are substantial differences between employers' obligations and liability in relation with each of those parties. The courts and the Internal Revenue Service (IRS) use certain criteria to determine whether an individual working for the company is an employee or an independent contractor; the employer's liability will be determined accordingly. When deciding which route to go for professional services, employers should know the differences in responsibility, liability, and loyalty.

Liability

The main concern of many business owners is the liability for the actions of their workers. In the employer/employee relationship, the employer has the right to control the manner of the employee's performance. Accordingly, the company is vicariously liable for the actions of the employee that are committed within the scope of employment. Notice that the stress is on the *right to* control, not on *actual* control. In other words, the employer is liable whether he or she controls the employee's actions or not. In the employer/independent contractor relationship, the employer does not control nor supervise the manner of the job performance; therefore, the employer is not liable for the independent contractor's misconduct. The exception is when the independent contractor was engaged in ultra-hazardous activity, in which case the employer may be liable. Activity is deemed ultra-hazardous when it is likely to cause damage to third parties due to the lack of proper precautions (for example, work on the construction sites, gas stations, etc.). In this case, courts hold employers and their independent contractors liable, in an effort to ensure that public safety will be observed at all times.

Termination of Relationships

The relationship between an employer and independent contractor is temporary in nature. Both parties negotiate their obligations and termination of their professional relationship before the start of the work. In the case of an employee, an employer may face claims for unlawful termination. The employee may claim he or she relied on company policy in relation to other employees, discrimination based on the membership in the protected class, retaliation, or wrongful termination in violation of other public policies. When courts hear wrongful termination claims, the standard of review is fairness. Would a jury, without any knowledge regarding the personalities involved, find that the termination was justified and the employee was treated fairly? Such litigation process can be very time consuming and costly.

Payment for Services

Independent contractors are paid an agreed-upon amount on a per-project basis, for work actually performed. If the job is not satisfactorily done, the employer is entitled to terminate their relationship. On the contrary, under certain circumstances, employees can have a lawful right to take a medical or family leave and will be entitled to return to his or her previous or equivalent position once the medical or family situation has changed. Also, the Equal Pay Act (EPA) requires that women and men receive equal pay for equal work and that the employer cannot discriminate between employees on the basis of sex. The Fair Labor Standards Act (FLSA) governs wage and hour requirements. State labor laws have similar provisions to the FLSA, establishing the minimum wage and number of work hours. Independent contractors are not covered by the various state and federal employment laws. Accordingly, they cannot claim their entitlement to something they have not bargained for.

Taxes

Employers must withhold income tax and pay unemployment insurance, workers' compensation insurance, Medicare, Social Security, and payroll taxes for every employee., They do not bear these obligations in the case of independent contractors. Sometimes, it is more beneficial for the employers to have a job done by an independent contractor rather than to hire an employee. This may be a way to cut labor costs without sacrificing productivity.

However, as I mentioned before, courts and the IRS utilize certain guidelines to determine whether a worker is an employee or an independent contractor. Improper classification of workers is risky. In past years employer misclassifications of independent contractors has cost the federal and state government billions of dollars in tax revenue. Thus, there is a renewed interest by government agencies in collecting payroll taxes and enforcing employment laws against companies that improperly classify their workers as independent contractors. To combat this problem, federal and state agencies have allotted much bigger budgets for auditing companies. Improper worker classification can lead to administrative audits, assessments, fines, penalties, and litigation.

There are no strict lines to differentiate employees from independent contractors, but in reviewing the employment status of a particular individual the following basic characteristics are applied:

• Generally, an individual is an employee if the employer controls the manner of his or her work and the means used to achieve results. With an independent contractor, an employer may only control or direct the final outcome of the work, not the way job is performed. For example, an employee works from the employer's space using the employer's technology; an independent contractor organizes the working conditions him- or herself and delivers the final product to the employer. The employer does not control the time, place, and method of independent contractor's performance.

• The employer pays commissions or per-job fee to the independent contractor rather than an hourly wage or salary, such as are paid to employees. The contractor will be compensated for work completed rather than for hours worked. The employer also does not provide fringe benefits (medical and life insurance, participation in the pension plans, etc.) to contractors.

• Independent contractors usually have some indicia of independent business, such as business cards, websites, their own support personnel, and consultants.

• The employer cannot restrict the independent contractor from performing services for others while working for that employer.

• The contractor must be able to make important business decisions by him- or herself (for example, whether to hire assistants, what equipment to use, where to do the job, etc.).

Just as employees so independent contractors can bind the company to certain liabilities if they act as agents of the company. Most contracts entered by the agents on behalf of the company are enforceable. Also, the company is responsible for the actions of its agents, as long as those actions fall within the scope of their employment relationship. A well-drafted written agreement with each party, stating a detailed job description and what one is authorized to do on behalf of the company in various situations is paramount in the successful management.

CHAPTER 5

Intellectual Property

Trademarks/Servicemarks

Entrepreneurs put much effort, time, and money into establishing and developing their businesses. After creating something special, they want to be sure they and those approved by them will be the only beneficiaries of their hard work. They also want to be distinguishable from their competitors. For this reason, companies and sole proprietors create trademarks and servicemarks and conduct commercial activities under them.

A trademark is any word, letter, name, slogan, symbol, design, logo, shape, image, sound, color, or combination thereof that is used or intended to be used in commerce. In short, it is a brand name. Trademark relates to goods, while servicemark relates to provided services. The same law protects both.

Why to use a trademark/servicemark?

• to identify and distinguish one company's goods or services from those of other sellers or manufacturers;

• to demonstrate to consumers and clients that all the products or services come from the same source (a certain company);

• to signify to consumers and clients that all the products or services are of equal quality.

The Trademark and Copyright Law states that trademark ownership rights arise from the use ("first in use, first in right"). Therefore, priority and ownership are governed by who wins the race to the marketplace, not by the first one to arrive at the U.S. Patent and Trademark Office (USPTO). Registration with USPTO does not grant ownership. It is important because it proves the validity of the trademark/servicemark ownership and affords additional protection and advantages to the trademarks owners, something common law does not provide.

Very often, people contribute substantial work and financial resources to market, promote, and establish goodwill with their customers and clients. Registration of their trademarks helps companies avoid unfair competition, protects trademarks owners' rights, and grants further benefits in using their trademarks. The registration of the trademark/servicemark with USPTO:

• grants to the trademark owners exclusive nationwide rights to use the mark on or in connection with the goods/services set forth in the registration and execute licenses to others for its use at the owners' discretion;

• gives constructive nationwide notice of the trademark owners' rights (the mark shows up in trademark searches);

• can be used as a basis for obtaining registration in foreign countries;

• may be filed with U.S. Customs Service to prevent exportation of infringing goods to foreign countries;

• helps to prevent others from taking advantage of the trademark publicity by infringing the original mark, counterfeiting, operating under similar or confusing marks, or committing other actions that may be detrimental to the trademarks owners;

• enables to sue for infringement and invoke jurisdiction of federal courts;

• affords legal presumption of the validity of the mark and its owners' rights in court;
• allows for claim of statutory treble damages, disgorgement of profits, and costs for willfulness;

• allows the use of the registered symbol (®) to indicate exclusive ownership rights; and

• overall, is an incontestable evidence of trade/servicemark ownership.

The U.S. Trademark and Copyright Law and the USPTO's mission is to ensure that the intellectual property system contributes to a strong global economy, encourages investments in innovation, and fosters entrepreneurial spirit. It promotes industrial and technological progress in the United States and strengthens the national economy.

Copyrights

In order to promote the progress of science and useful arts and to give people incentive to create and commercially leverage their works, U.S. Copyright Law protects the exclusive rights of the creators of the copyrighted work.

Copyright Law protects the original work of authorship fixed in tangible mediums of expression. In other words, in order to be protected, the work must be:

1. created by the author seeking to register it (created independently);

2. original (not copied from somewhere in whole or in part);

3. creative (not a plain compilation of information);

4. fixed in a tangible mediums of expression (not merely an idea or plan to create in the future); and

5. non-utilitarian in nature (Copyright protects only expression, not function. Functions are protected by Patent Law).

An idea itself is not protectable until it is put into a tangible form. The works protected by Copyright Law include:

• Literary works

• Musical works

• Dramatic works

• Pantomimes and choreographic works

- Pictorial, graphic and sculptural works

- Motion pictures and other audiovisual works

- Sound recordings

- Architectural works

- Vessel hulls

Copyright Law grants and protects only certain rights of the original author, as listed below:

- Right to reproduce the work

- Right to prepare derivative works

- Right to distribute copies of the work to public (sell, lease)

- Right to perform the work publicly

- Right to display the work publicly

- Right to perform the work by means of a digital audio transmission (for sound recordings)

The ownership rights are not automatically perpetual in nature. The law grants ownership to the creator and his or her heirs during a definite period of time. Copyright Law protects the author's ownership of the work during the author's lifetime, plus seventy years thereafter. If the work was made for hire or it is created anonymously, the protection of copyright is either for 95 years from the moment of its first display or 120 years from its creation, whichever is shorter. Heirs can renew and prolong their ownership rights before the expiration of the initial protection period, but if no such action is made, the copyrighted work becomes public domain and is available for public use. We enjoy today many great works that became public domain because copyrights for them were not timely claimed. Agood example are multiple Christmas songs and movies we regularly hear and watch during the holiday season. They are royalties and licenses free and for this reason are translated over and over through multiple channels.

Copyright is a personal property right, and its owner may use it just as they would any other personal property: selling, licensing, granting, including it in a will, offering it as collateral, using it as business capital, and in any other conceivable way. A very popular way to earn profits on a created property and to promote the work beyond individual's personal efforts is to license the work to others for any specific use. The license can be temporary or permanent, exclusive or non-exclusive (authorizing several people to use the work at the same time), and the author can include any other provisions he or she desires.

The copyright owner cannot stop others from using the work altogether, for there are certain exceptions to copyright infringement. The copyrighted work of others is not infringed if it is used for fair purpose, also known as "fair use". Fair use is determined based on the following factors:

- purpose and character of the use (commercial vs. not-for-profit, such as a book used for educational purposes);

- nature of copyrighted work;

- amount and substantiality of the portion used in relation to copyrighted work as a whole (the main part of the work or just a short excerpt);

• impact of the use on the market value of the work (how much the unauthorized use influences the ability of the owner to distribute his work at the marker and its price).

Another exception to copyright infringement is the "first sale" doctrine, which states that the owner of a particular copy of the work can sell or dispose of that copy without the copyright owner's permission. For example, if a person purchases a book or disc, they may later resell that item with no risk of infringement. An infringer, on the other hand, would be someone who creates and then distributes multiple copies of the original work without permission from the copyright holder.

Ownership of copyright automatically vests in its creator unless work was made for hire. If it is a work-for-hire situation, the person who ordered the work's creation is considered to be the owner. The commissioning party of the work is deemed to be the author.

Although the creator does not have to register his or her work to establish ownership, official registration with U.S. Copyright Office is highly advisable. Registration is a legal formality intended to create a public record of the basic facts pertaining to the copyright. The registration can be filed at any time during the life of copyright, but the sooner the better. Registration of copyright confers several significant advantages on copyright owners:

• It creates public record of owner's copyright.

• Without proper registration it can be challenging for the owner to prove anywhere that the initial creation of the work belongs to him.

• Registration is required to bring a lawsuit in U.S. Federal courts.

• If registration is made within five years of public display of the work, it establishes *prima facie* evidence of copyright validity and facts stated in the registration certificate.

• In case of infringement, the claimant must have a duly registered work to qualify for statutory damages and attorney fees. While in the case of copyright violation, actual damages may not be significant (if the claimant did not lose big profits from work being unlawfully used by others), statutory damages are high, and the threat of them can stop many parties from unfair business practices. For example, provided that the claimant did not sustain a great loss, the statutory damages awarded under normal circumstances may be up to $30,000, or $30,000 to $150,000 for willful infringement

• Registration allows the copyright owner to have U.S. Customs prohibit importation of infringing copies of the work.

Whether the work is registered or not, the owner should use reasonable means to indicate copyright ownership to others. A simple way to do this is to place the copyright symbol (©) followed by the date of creation and the owner's name on each piece of the displayed work. This notice informs the public that the work is protected by Copyright Law, shows when it was first created, identifies the copyright owner, and will counter any attempted defense of innocent infringement.

Copyright Law favors creators and greatly protects them from infringement, but it is not always automatic. Copyright owners must make reasonable efforts to protect their copyrights, including proper and timely registration of the work with U.S. Copyright office, timely notification to other parties of rights when infringements are detected, careful monitoring, taking necessary precautions when entering into business relation-ships with other parties (e.g. not allowing them to use the copyrighted work without execution of a proper license agree-ment), not allowing others to make derivatives from the work without express written authorization, and other measures that may be dictated by the particular situations. If the copyright owner does not properly protect the work, rights may be lost due to bad business practices of others and the owner's in-ability to prove that he or she did not accept and ratify such practices by his inactivity. The bright side is that the creator's ownership rights are well protected once registered and grant-ed to others only with the existence of a duly executed license agreement.

Trade Secrets

So many of the things we enjoy today started with nothing more than a good idea. Great business empires have been built because of successful business principles and strategies. Many generations benefit from someone's original contribution. In-novation is a key to dynamic economy. Sound public policy seeks to encourage invention of new products, processes, and technologies; promote innovation; prevent unfair competition; and generally benefit our society. This is all vital to the devel-opment and success of the business. Thus, there is a concomi-tant need to protect and exploit the fruits of intellectual labor and thus ensure their continued creation.

U.S. Intellectual Property Law strictly protects the rights of intellectual property owners. At the same time, some of the largest reported business claims in recent years have arisen as a result of trade secrets misappropriation. Many such claims involve business relationships that have gone bad.

The creators of the intellectual property, such as trademarks/ servicemarks, copyrights, patents, and domain names, can officially register and put the world on notice about their exclusive ownership rights to the said. The situation is more complicated when it comes to invisible trade secrets and business ideas, which are also fall under the category of the intellectual property. First, only things that are put into a tangible form can be registered; accordingly, an idea cannot be registered. Second, everything that is registered becomes publically known and will no longer remain a secret, the complete opposite of what trade secret and unique business idea owners want. The firms and entrepreneurs want to protect their secrets and information or technology they create or develop in case it is both confidential and commercially valuable. The trade secrets law protects these assets against unauthorized acquisition, use, or disclosure by others.

Almost any information used in the course of business can be protected as a trade secret. This might include formulas; manufacturing techniques; product specifications; customer lists; information related to merchandising, costs, and pricing; internal company practices; and any new business-related ideas. Very often, entrepreneurs cannot move forward with their ideas without the assistance of others such as employees, independent contractors, partners, or investors. The question is how to get other people onboard and protect the confidential nature of the information at the same time. While trade secrets owners escape the initial rigors of the official registration process, they must focus on installing contractual and other safeguards to maintain the confidential status of the shared information.

The rule of thumb is to know precisely to whom trade secrets are disclosed and to disclose them no more broadly that intended. Limit disclosure to those on a need-to-know basis. Once the proposed recipients of the confidential information are identified, the disclosing party should require each individual recipient (not a company in general) who has access to key information to enter into a non-disclosure agreement. This agreement binds the parties to keep certain business information that they may obtain during their involvement with the firm or entrepreneur as a secret and prevents them from disclosing it to the trade secrets owners' competitors or to the general public. In a non-disclosure agreement, the disclosing party should include:

- the detailed definition of confidential information;

- the purpose for which the information is being disclosed and the list of situations in which it may be used;

- the time period of confidentiality;

- the term (in years) during which the agreement is binding;

- the obligations of the recipient regarding the confidential information, such as to use it for enumerated purposes, to use reasonable efforts to keep it secure, to ensure that anyone to whom the information is disclosed will further abide by the same obligations as contained in their agreement;

- types of permissible disclosure, such as those required by law or court order.

In the case of prospective investors and partners, the receiving party may be unwilling to even consider entering into a non-disclosure agreement before they are aware that the proposed information will hold any value for them. What to do in this case? Business discussions often proceed in stages. Trade secrets owners may present the information in two portions. Limited information, which does not give away substantial details (such as a generic description of the project), may be disclosed initially so parties can evaluate whether it makes sense to form an ongoing relationship. Then, if interest arises, more information may be disclosed upon signing of a non-disclosure agreement. If, after disclosing a trade secret, the relationship between the parties does not progress for any reason or comes to an end because the purpose of the relationship has been fulfilled (e.g. termination of someone's employment), the disclosing party must ensure that that all confidential information is returned or destroyed and that the receiving party will continue to be under the obligation not to disclose or use the information in the future for its own or others benefits. Addressing such issues in early contractual documents before they become stark realities will frequently make for a smoother breakup.

Much of trade secrets law focuses on the risks that employees, former or prospective business partners, and various affiliates can pose to trade secrets. Thoughtful diligence in identifying potential recipients of the confidential information, controlling and documenting disclosures, and establishing contractual and practical safeguards to prevent unauthorized use or disclosure can help prevent trade secrets misappropriation, acquisition by accident or mistake, wrongful taking, unauthorized use, misunderstandings and disputes between the parties.

Licenses

The owner of the intellectual property (IP), whether copyright, trademark, or patent, is entitled to take full advantage of that creation or acquisition. First of all, the owner has an exclusive right to use the work unrestrictedly and develop future products and services based upon it. He or she can legally prohibit others from using the work without his or her express authorization. Most often, the future development, exploration, and utilization of the IP work will be limited if its owner relies solely on his or her personal capabilities and resources. Also, not everyone will be interested in further exploration of his or her own intellectual property; or it could be that while a person owns IP, a third party may be better suited to commercialize and monetize it. Even if the involvement of IP owner stops with the initial creation and registration of the work, or if the owner decides to involve other professionals in order to promote it, he or she can derive substantial benefits and generate royalty revenues from it, as long as the work has some value to others. This is where all kinds of licenses come into the picture, allowing the IP owner to become a licensor.

While licensing affords certain benefits to the licensor, it is an effective business model from the licensees' perspective as well. A party may prefer to license a product or technology that it can utilize in its business operations rather than to construct one by themselves; this may allow them to save time and money. Also, the business may not have the necessary time or other resources to create the product it needs. A licensee may also accept a license proposal for very practical reasons, such as avoiding a lawsuit for infringement or avoiding being precluded from using an essential technology. Licenses can also be an important element in joint ventures or projects in which two or more parties are collaborating, and they have to share the product of their work in order to reach a mutual goal.

A license is permission from the IP owner to another party to use or do certain things with his or her IP. Any form of intellectual property can be licensed. Copyrights are licensed for music, books, movies, and other written works. Trademarks are licensed for franchising, endorsements, cross-promotions, and merchandise deals. Trade secrets are licensed in dealings between companies or individuals seeking to work together and sharing confidential information in order to accomplish their projects. Rights of publicity are licensed by individuals in endorsement deals, advertising, and marketing.

Each form of IP has certain associated rights. These rights can be licensed together to one person or separately to different parties. The owner of copyright can license one party to reproduce the work, the other to publicly display the work, the third to include the part of the work in that party's other project, the forth to distribute or produce variations of the work, and so on. The owner of IP has almost unlimited ability to divide these rights and the work itself and license each piece separately. For example, separate chapters of a book can be licensed to different people for different reasons - one licensee is allowed to include the chapter in his or her own materials, while another is authorized to create a screenplay based on that book's chapter. The licensor can draft a license agreement as broadly or as narrowly as desired. The licensee will be able to use only the pieces of the work named in the license agreement and only for the indicated purposes. Also, the owner can issue both exclusive and nonexclusive license. The latter means the owner can issue exactly the same license to multiple parties. Ownership of the IP remains with the licensor, and only certain rights are conveyed to the licensee.

A license is a legally binding agreement, and its terms are strictly enforced by the courts. The licensor should be very careful not to give away rights he or she intends to keep and not to expose him- or herself to liability because of the actions of his licensees in the course of using the product or service. Drafting a license agreement requires consideration of many issues, both presently known and anticipated in the future; together, these form the scope of the license. Each of these elements, if not properly addressed, may bring unfavorable consequences on the licensee, the licensor, or both. The most common problem is that the scope of the license is not clearly and specifically identified. Parties mistakenly offer only broad, general description to what is licensed and do not indicate all possible uses. Then arguments may arise that one party exceeded the scope of the license. This may result in protracted and expensive litigation and in the licensor losing substantial profits, unable to collect the dues or to license the same rights to others. Another example is when rights are granted to the particular licensee without saying more. In the future, the licensee may be acquired by another company, and the acquiring company may end up with the license rights that the licensor never intended to grant in the first place. Such oversights may prove to be very detrimental to the licensor.

Other important issues to consider when licensing are:

- The scope of the grant: What can the licensee do with the licensed IP and for what purpose?

- Where can the license be exercised? What is the geographical scope of the license?

- Can the licensee assign the license or sublicense IP? If so, for what purposes?

- Is it exclusive or nonexclusive?

- How long is the license valid? Is it perpetual or temporary?

- Is the license terminable or irrevocable?

- What is the process of returning the licensed materials once the license expires?

- License payments and audit rights: Is it a one-time payment or are there ongoing royalties?

Flat fee payments or varying amounts based on profits?

- Are developments, extensions, and derivative works of the licensed product allowed, and

who will have the ownership interest?

- Are warranties and indemnification included? (For example, a warranty that the licensed product will comply with the representations and descriptions; a warranty that its use will not infringe any third-party IP rights; in case any claims arise from the use of the licensed product, who is entitled to indemnity and up to what amount).

The list above is far from being exhaustive, but it is a demonstration of the key issues in licensing. The drafting of licenses will vary greatly, depending on the materials being licensed and the interests of all involved parties. The IP owner can be restricted in using his or her own IP if he or she grants a poorly drafted license that does not explicitly state the licensee's and licensor's rights and obligations and other essential terms. Moreover, the law does not require that the license be in writing. Courts may consider the course of business dealings and relationships between the parties in order to determine whether the license agreement existed and whether it is proven by the prior conduct of the parties. For example, if one party is using the IP of another with the IP owner's knowledge for some time and the IP owner claims he or she did not authorize the first party to do so, the court may determine that the license existed based on the fact that the IP owner knew about such use and did not object in a timely fashion. As the main value of IP rights is in their exploitation, it is vitally important to have a well-written, all-inclusive, specific, unambiguous license agreement with every person who may use an IP product, be it for a short or long period of time.

CHAPTER 6

Real Estate

Leasing

If an entrepreneur is not going to conduct business from his or her place of living, most likely a decision will have to be made about leasing an office, store, or storage space. The land-lord/tenant relationship is multifaceted and a long-term one. Accordingly, the leasing process can be complex and arduous. A commercial real estate lease is a long document, bringing together numerous rights and obligations of the parties in an attempt to govern their long-term relationships and to foresee various situations that may emerge in the future. U.S. law strict-ly enforces contractual agreements between parties. Therefore, it is essential to have a lease agreement in place that covers in detail even the most remote circumstances. Full discussion of the lease review process would require several volumes, but below, I will briefly review some of the most significant points in lease negotiations.

Premises: This is the area the rent price is based on. What are you paying for? For total square footage or usable square footage? Usable square footage excludes such common areas as elevators, stairways, halls, and the like. Landlords often market space as available square feet, including allocation of various common areas within the available premises. Thus, rentable and usable measurements may be different.

Are the premises suitable for intended use? When determining if the premises are suitable for intended use, consideration should be given not only to present, but also to tenant's possible future needs (possibility of establishment of a different business on the same premises, optional expansion, rent price on additional expanded space, etc.).

Term: Beyond the obvious need to address the duration of the tenancy, the parties should discuss the possibilities of lease extension and/or termination and the date of the lease commencement. The tenant will want the lease to commence once the business can be feasibly conducted; if the building is under construction and the lease commences immediately, the tenant may be stuck with useless space.

Base Rent: The base rental price may be net or gross rental. Gross rental means the tenant will be paying a *pro rata* portion of all operating expenses and real estate taxes, in addition to the net rent. Various other charges may be included in the rent (utility charges are common example). In some cases, it may be cheaper for the tenant to obtain these services independently rather than through the landlord. The more extra components are included in the rent, the more difficult it is for the tenant to verify costs and make sure that no third party is making a profit on services or products provided. The object of direct service agreements is to eliminate a middleman.

Landlord's and Tenant's Work. Alterations and Repairs:
The responsibility for present and future alterations and repairs should be allocated between the parties in advance. If the need arises to change the design or add new features to the space, to what extent the tenant is permitted to do so? Which alterations will be done at the tenant's expense and which at the landlord's? What decisions can the tenant make without the landlord's approval? To whom will the removable improvements of the space will belong after the lease is terminated? Also, during the period of tenancy, who is responsible for various necessary repairs?

Overall Condition of the Premises, Compliance with Laws, Insurance: Latent or hidden conditions may exist that are not obvious upon a walkthrough of the premises, and they may disturb the tenant's work on the premises. Environmental hazards are one example. Thus, the tenant should require the landlord to submit the results of the most recent examination of the premises and ensure that any hazardous conditions that may emerge in the future will be properly addressed. Also, it should be described in detail in the lease agreement what party will be held responsible for legal compliance costs, such as satisfaction of fire safety requirements, emergency lighting, the Americans with Disability Act, etc. The tenant should also ask to review the landlord's insurance policy in order to determine whether the space and the tenant's products will be adequately covered by it in various situations; if the landlord's insurance is not adequate, the tenant should obtain independent insurance. The tenant should also determine whether or not the landlord has sufficient coverage to pay for restoration of the premises in case of unforeseen circumstances, like a fire or flood.

Services: What services are included in the lease, if any? What does the tenant require? Does the tenant have flexibility in choosing services and providers? Does the landlord guarantee that the tenant will have these services continuously throughout the lease term? For example, what electrical voltage is necessary for the tenant's operations? Does the tenant require elevators, a separate phone line, cleaning services, air-conditioning and heating after business hours, parking, and building access during off hours? All of these things and more should be considered.

Assignment and Subletting: The parties should negotiate whether the tenant has a right to assign or sublet the space in whole or in part and whether he will need to obtain an additional approval from the landlord for each proposed sublease agreement.

Subordination and Non-Disturbance Provisions: The present landlord's interest in the premises may change in the future. Thus, the tenant should make a concerted effort to ensure that a change in building ownership will not affect the tenancy. The landlord may want to be able to sell the building free and clear from others' rights in order to attract more buyers. The parties must reach a compromise on this issue.

Personal Guarantees and Credit Consideration: Very often, the parties to the lease agreement are business entities rather than individuals. In such case, if one party defaults on its contractual obligations the damages of the injured party are limited by the amount of business assets and available insurance. Absent more, the tenant or the landlord may be left only with a claim against whatever capital the company has. Thus, the parties should consider one another's creditworthiness and, in case the business does not have enough capital or there is a risk of its diminishment, personal guarantees of its owners may be useful.

Defaults and Disputes: The parties should negotiate in advance the remedies that will be utilized in case of default. For example, the tenant may want the landlord to provide a period to cure default before filing a complaint with the court. As the landlord/tenant relationship is a long-term one, the parties should recognize the need for efficient and cost-effective dispute resolution mechanisms. A protracted litigation is detrimental to both parties and can be substituted by simpler, quicker methods of resolutions, such as arbitration, mediation, and other alternative dispute resolution procedures.

The process of lease negotiation may be lengthy and tedious, but only a carefully drafted, detail-oriented agreement can yield desired results and protect from unexpected surprises.

Buying

Rather than leasing, business owners may wish to buy commercial real estate as a place of operation for their companies or for investment purposes. It can be any commercial space, such as an office, store, warehouse, restaurant, or other. Prospective buyers should determine, considering their resources, the type of business, and probability of future profits, whether it is better to buy or lease a space for the commercial activities. The main advantage of buying real estate is obvious - it becomes an asset of the company or of the individual investor. Real estate owners are free to exploit their properties, observing national and local laws and regulations, but being totally independent of any private third party demands (e.g. restrictions imposed by a landlord). Choosing and buying commercial real estate substantially differs from buying a residential property. There is much to be considered in identifying a suitable property and before making a purchase offer.

Interests Transfer: When buying commercial real estate, the buyer may want to purchase not only a particular space, but also to have other interests transferred from the seller. For example, if there are tenants on the property, a prospective buyer may want to have leases assigned to him or her, entitling the buyer to continue rent collection from the existing tenants rather than looking for new occupants. Another example is the transfer of certain licenses that allow the buyer to continue using the property in its present capacity.

Number of Participants: There may be more parties involved than the buyer and a seller. If the property is leased, the rights of the tenants should be considered, particularly whether it is possible to revoke or make changes to their leases. If the seller has liens against the property, what are the rights and interests of the lienors? Is it possible to satisfy them before closing? If a seller has mortgage on the property, there may be several mortgagors; in this case, it is necessary to obtain an agreement from each of them prior to closing. The negotiations with all parties who may have some interest in the real property may be extensive, but it is vitally important to find out their positions before proceeding with the transaction.

Property Ownership: The property may be owned by an individual, private company, non-for-profit corporation, or any other legal entity. The identity and type of the property owner can affect the transaction in terms of taxation and liability. If a property owner is not a U.S. taxpayer, this will also affect the transaction.

Property Value: The value of the commercial property is not only in its purchase price, but also in the amount of prospective income it might generate over time. Accordingly, it is very important to make sure that the property can be used for conducting regular business activities. Buyers should consider insurance policies not only against risk of loss due to natural disasters or other casualties, but also against the loss of income due to business interruption or against liability that may arise from property use by the licensees or invitees.

Compliance with Securities Laws: If the interests in real estate at issue may be offered to general public for the investment opportunities, such transactions fall under the Securities and Exchange Commission (SEC) regulation and require certain public disclosures.

Federal, State, and Local Health, Safety, and Environmental Regulations: Commercial properties are subject to various regulations intended to protect safety and health of general public and environment.

Americans with Disabilities Act (ADA) Compliance: The buyer must inquire about past renovations and determine whether the building is subject to the Act and meets all ADA standards.

Due Diligence: Prior to signing a contract of sale, the buyer must perform certain due diligence to verify whether the property is suitable for use and in compliance with the seller's representations or lack of such. The seller has an obligation to disclose some conditions, albeit not all. It is the buyer's responsibility to conduct all necessary investigations before purchasing any property, particularly the following:

1. The first main item is the title to the property. The buyer's attorney should perform title search to ensure that the seller is the true and legal owner of the property and that his or her ownership, interests, and the right to transfer the property is not restricted by the interests of any third parties.

2. The buyer should ensure that the seller transfers exactly what was agreed upon. The parties may want either to use the recent survey of the property or order a new survey if it is outdated. A licensed land surveyor should visit the property and will draw a map of the land, indicating the exact boundaries of the land being conveyed, who owns the adjacent parcels of the land from all sides, whether there are easements and covenants attached to the land, and, if they are, which portions of the land are affected by them, as well as various other information needed to precisely identify the property being transferred.

3. The buyer's attorney should obtain proof that all charges payable in connection with the property (which can become liens against the property if unpaid), are satisfied by the seller.

4. The buyer's attorney should check existing and potential zoning regulations to make sure the buyer will be able to use the property as intended. Zoning regulations are imposed by the local government and list the purposes for which the land may be used (e.g. exclusively residential area, commercial area, or a combination of these). If current zoning code does not permit the buyer to use the property as desired, the parties may agree to apply to the local zoning authority to obtain approval for the proposed use as a condition of the sale. Failure to understand zoning codes may be very costly to the buyer, as it may prevent intended use of the property after the purchase. Zoning requirements also significantly affect the marketability of the property.

5. The buyer should make inquiries whether the property is located within a historic preservation district. In some areas, the rights of the owners to change the façade of the building are limited by the enacted legislation that aims to

preserve the architectural heritage. This may be a concern for an owner who wants to remodel the building to a more modern look; in this case, the new owner needs to obtain an approval from the Landmarks Preservation Commission before making any changes.

6. The buyer may want to retain an engineer or architect to examine the property for physical problems. Often serious physical problems may not be evident to the casual observer. These can include problems with the roof, foundation, supporting structures, utility systems, and architectural defects. In addition, the buyer may wish to perform environmental examinations of the grounds and structures to exclude the possibility of toxic substances being released or stored on the premises.

When all due diligence matters are completed and the parties have necessary information about each other and the property to be transferred, they can begin negotiations of the contract of sale. Contracts for the purchase of commercial properties are often very lengthy and complex documents, drafted and negotiated by attorneys for the respective parties. Various terms may be negotiated in connection with the purchase of real estate. The partial example of negotiable items are purchase price, down payment, mortgage, personal property included in the price of the real property, repairs to be made before the closing date, risk of loss, the rights of the existing tenants (if any), damages in case any of the parties fails to promptly proceed with the transaction, and so on.

If the buyer needs financing to make a purchase, then the buyer must apply for and obtain a commitment letter from his prospective lender before closing. If the buyer does not have any other means to buy a property other than a loan, the contract of sale must be contingent on the buyer's ability to obtain such financing. After signing the contract of sale and before the closing, the buyer must make good-faith, diligent efforts to obtain financing on the prevalent terms. If the seller has mortgage against the property, he or she must make arrangements with his or her existing mortgagor to have the mortgage satisfied or assigned to the buyer on the date of the closing. Many financial institutions make the satisfaction of the mortgage a condition precedent to selling the property.

The closing date is when all pre-closing conditions are satisfied and parties, their attorneys, and other interested participants meet to transfer the title of the property from the seller to the buyer. The seller delivers the deed and keys to the buyer, the buyer pays the balance of the purchase price to the seller, the representative of the title company issues a new title insurance policy on the buyer's name assuring the buyer that proper title is being delivered, and the real estate brokers are paid their commissions if they assisted with the transaction. If the seller has a mortgage on the property or the buyer is going to obtain financing, the representatives of the lending institutions will also be present. After the parties exchange all necessary documents and sign transfer taxes forms, the new owner can begin exploring the property and enjoying his or her new possession.

CHAPTER 7

Taxation

As anyone who has ever filled out a tax return knows, the U.S. tax system is very complex. Therefore, this chapter aims to provide a basic overview and highlights the main provisions.

U.S. taxes are imposed on two levels, federal and state, and sometimes a third—local, such as city or county. At the federal level, there is income tax, including corporate and personal income tax, capital gains tax, income tax on dividends, interest and royalties, taxes on partnership profits, and employee payroll taxes. State-level taxes are generally similar to federal, only at much lower rates (0 to 10 percent), plus sales and use taxes. Some counties and cities have their own unique tax regimes, such as income and business taxes and property taxes if a business is located and operated within their territories.

Corporations and individuals are taxed, and the type and amount of taxes a businessperson has to pay will depend on the structure of his business. Sole proprietors and partnerships are not taxed on the entity level, and business income, expenses, and deductions flow directly to the owners. They report their business income on their individual income tax returns and are personally responsible for paying taxes. These types of business structures are called pass-through entities for tax purposes. However, the partnership has to file informational income tax return, even if it does not pay taxes on its own. Corporations, on the other hand, are taxed on the entity level first, as they are considered independent business structures fully separate from their owners (shareholders). If the profits are distributed as dividends to the shareholders, the shareholders have to pay additional taxes on their individual income (current federal rate on such dividend income is 15 percent). In this sense, corporations are double-taxed, as compared to other business entities. The legal entity known as an S corporation allows small corporations with less than 100 shareholders, all of whom are individuals (not other business entities) and residents of a particular state in which that corporation is formed to be taxed as a partnership. All income of S corporation passes through the entity to its shareholders, and they are personally responsible for filing and paying taxes. S corporation does not pay taxes as an entity. The members of Limited Liability Company (LLC) have an option to choose whether their company will be taxed as a corporation or as a partnership. Single-member LLC is automatically taxed as a partnership. Its members pay income taxes, not the company. LLC with several members can be taxed as its members prefer. If the LLC is taxed as a partnership, LLC members are taxed on allocations, not distributions of income. This means they must file and pay taxes on the generated income, even if it is not distributed, but left in the company for future expenses and development.

Income Tax

Generally, all business entities, irrespective of their legal structure, must file an annual tax return. They (or their owners, in the case of a pass-through entity) also have to file quarterly tax returns and make estimated tax payments if they expect to own taxes of more than $1,000 per quarter. Corporations have to make estimated tax payments if they expect to owe tax of $500 or more when they file their returns. U.S. taxes are calculated based on taxable income, gross income earned by the taxpayer minus allowable deductions and adjustments. The most common deductions are various business expenses, losses, depreciation, interest, wages, contributions to the employee benefits plans, state and local taxes, and other operating costs of running a business. The applicable tax rates depend on the net taxable income. The current rates for the individuals who report business profits on their personal income tax returns are as follows:

Tax Rate--Single Taxpayers—2012

Taxable income:

Over	But not over	Tax	+%	On amount over
$0	$8,700	$0.00	10	$0
8,700	35,350	870.00	15	8,700
35,350	85,650	4,867.50	25	35,350
85,650	178,650	17,442.50	28	85,650
178,650	388,350	43,482.50	33	178,650
388,350	& above	112,683.50	35	388,350

Tax Rates--Married Individuals Filing Joint and Surviving Spouses—2012

Taxable income: *Tax:*

Over	But not over	Tax	+%	On amount over
$0	$17,400	$0.00	10	$0
17,4 00	70,700	1,740.00	15	17,400
70,700	142,700	9,735.00	25	70,700
142,700	217,450	27,735.00	28	142,700
217,450	388,350	48,665.00	33	217,450
388,350	& above	105,062.00	35	388,350

Tax Rates--Married Individuals Filing Separate—2012

Taxable income: *Tax:*

Over	But not over	Tax	+%	On amount over
$0	$8,700	$0.00	10	$0
8,700	35,350	870.00	15	8,700
35,350	71,350	4,867.50	25	35,350
71,350	108,725	13,867.50	28	71,350
108,725	194,175	24,332.50	33	108,725
194,175	& above	52,531.00	35	194,175

Tax Rates--Heads Of Households—2012

Taxable income: *Tax:*

Over	But not over	Tax	+%	On amount over
$0	$12,400	$0.00	10	$0
12,400	47,350	1,240.00	15	12,400
47,350	122,300	6,482.50	25	47,350
122,300	198,050	25,220.00	28	122,300
198,050	388,350	46,430.00	33	198,050
388,350	& above	109,229.00	35	388,350

Current corporate rates are as follows:

Taxable income over	But not over	Tax rate
$0	$50,000	15%
50,000	75,000	25%
75,000	100,000	34%
100,000	335,000	39%
335,000	10,000,000	34%
10,000,000	15,000,000	35%
15,000,000	18,333,333	38%
18,333,333	& above	35%

Alternative Minimum Tax (AMT)

Alternative minimum tax is a flat-rate income tax imposed by the United States federal government on individuals, corporations, estates, and trusts rather than regular income tax when an adjusted amount of taxable income is above a certain threshold. If the application of an AMT results in a higher tax than the regular income tax, AMT is imposed instead of the regular income tax. As with regular federal income tax, rates and exemptions of AMT vary by filing status, but they are completely different from regular income tax. Currently, the lowest AMT rate is 25 percent of taxable income. The AMT is intended to ensure that U.S. taxpayers with substantial economic income pay at least a minimum amount of tax, notwithstanding exclusions, deductions, and credits otherwise available by law.

A corporation is exempt from AMT during its first year as a company. Further, corporations with average annual gross receipts less than $7,500,000 for the prior three years are exempt from AMT, but only so long as they continue to meet this test.

Consolidated Tax Returns

A group of companies consisting of a U.S. parent company and subsidiaries, in which at least 80 percent of interest is owned by a parent company, may be taxed on their consolidated income, by filing a consolidated federal income tax return. In such case, the losses sustained by one subsidiary may be deducted from overall income and offset profits of other subsidiaries or a parent company, therefore lowering the amount of owned taxes. Also, the dividends paid by the affiliated companies to their parent company are exempt from U.S. federal income tax.

Capital Gains Tax

For corporations, the excess of net gains from the sale of capital assets over net losses from the sale of the assets or net capital gains are taxed at the same rates applicable to the ordinary income. Thus, the current maximum rate is 35 percent. However, capital losses may only be used to offset capital gains and the excess of losses over gains may be carried back three years or forward five years. Losses must be applied to the earliest carryback year before any carryforwards may be used. Gains or losses on the sale or exchange of capital assets held for more than twelve months are treated as long-term capital gains or losses. Gains or losses on the sale or exchange of capital assets held for twelve months or less are treated as short-term capital gains or losses.

Net Operating Loss Carryback/Carryforward

If a company has an operating loss in any year, this loss can be offset against prior income, as well as any future income. Generally, it can be carried back first to the two years preceding the loss year, then forward to the twenty years following the loss year. The taxpayer can, by filing an election, waive the entire carryback period, and the net operating loss can only be carried forward.

Self-Employment Tax

Self-employment tax is a Social Security and Medicare tax primarily for individuals who work for themselves. These tax payments contribute to such individuals' coverage under the

Social Security system. Social Security coverage provides the self-employed with retirement benefits, disability benefits, survivor benefits, and hospital insurance (Medicare) benefits. Individuals who earn more than $400 (or $108.28 if a church employee) have to pay this kind of tax.

Employment Taxes

When a company has employees, the employer bears the burden of certain employment tax responsibilities. The employer must withheld these taxes from each employee's salary, make a matching contribution itself, and submit the payment to the government on the employee's behalf. Employment taxes include the following:

Social Security and Medicare Taxes: The employer withholds part of these taxes from the employee's wages and pays another part of these taxes from the company's funds on every employee it has. (To find out how much Social Security and Medicare taxes to withhold and pay, see Publication 15 on www.irs.gov).

Federal Income Tax Withholding: The employer must generally withhold federal income tax from employee wages and submit it to the government. (To figure how much federal income tax to withhold from each wage payment, use the employee's Form W-4, Employee's Withholding Allowance Certificate, and the methods described in Publication 15 on www. irs.gov).

Federal Unemployment Tax (FUTA): The federal unemployment tax is part of the federal and state program under the Federal Unemployment Tax Act (FUTA) that pays unemployment compensation to workers who lose their jobs. The employer pays FUTA tax from its own funds. Employees do not pay this tax or have it withheld from their pay.

Once the calendar year is over, the employer must furnish copies of Form W-2, Wage and Tax Statement, to each employee to whom it paid wages during the preceding year and must also send copies to the Social Security Administration.

The company does not have to withhold or pay any taxes on payments made to an independent contractor, but as mentioned previously, tax authorities are very strict about companies observing the differences between the employees and independent contractors. If the employer improperly classifies an employee as an independent contractor, it can be held liable for employment taxes for that worker, in addition to huge penalties. An independent contractor is someone who is self-employed, retained by a company on a temporary basis for a particular kind of job assignment, and is otherwise fully independent of that company.

Excise Tax

Certain types of businesses have to pay excise taxes. These may be applicable if the company:

- manufactures or sells certain products;

- operates certain kinds of businesses;

- uses various kinds of equipment, facilities, or products; or

- receives payment for certain services.

Excise taxes consist of several broad categories of taxes, including the following.

- Environmental taxes

- Communications and air transportation taxes

- Fuel taxes

- Tax on the first retail sale of heavy trucks, trailers, and tractors

- Manufacturers taxes on the sale or use of a variety of different articles

For full description of commercial activities that are subject to excise taxes and their categories, see Publication 510 at: www.irs.gov/publications/p510/index.html

State Income Tax

In addition to federal taxes, nearly all U.S. states impose their own income tax. These are similar to federal taxes, but state tax is usually only applicable to income attributable to that particular state. There should be a nexus between the activities conducted in that state and derived income, a physical or business connection between a taxpayer and a state. A business that has an office, employees, or equipment in a state will be taxed by that state. If an individual lives or consistently works in a state, he or she will be considered a resident of that state for tax purposes. However, states can also tax individuals and entities based on other connections, such as frequent business visits. The rates differ from state to state and currently range from 1 to 10 percent.

A taxpayer may be exempt from the imposition of a state income tax if the activity it conducts within the state is limited to mere solicitation for business, such as advertisement. Businesses should take care when evaluating whether activities are protected under this rule, as mere solicitation has a very specific meaning; there is a fine line that must not be crossed. This solicitation exemption does not extend to other types of state and local taxes.

If a company has nexus in more than one state, its overall taxable income must be apportioned among the states based on its apportionment factors. Generally the amount of income taxes due in each particular state is based on the extent of the commercial activities conducted in that state.

State Sales and Use Taxes

States collect sales tax on retail sales within the state and use tax of varying rates in different locations. Companies are generally responsible for collecting these taxes, holding them as a trustee, then submitting them to the government. If the company is not doing business in a particular U.S. state, it is usually not obligated to collect sales tax on sales within that state.

Non-exempted tangible personal property purchased outside of the buyer's home state and brought back into it, on which the out-of-state seller has not collected sales tax at least equal to the home state's use tax, is subject to the home state use tax. Out-of-state purchases of tangible personal property intended for resale by the buyer are exempt from home state use tax; whereas, if it is for use or consumption by the buyer, it will apply (absent certain exemptions).

New York City Business Tax

Certain businesses located and conducting commercial activities in New York City may be subject to NYC corporate and unincorporated business tax.

Other State and Local Taxes

State and local jurisdictions may impose many additional types of taxes, fees, and other filing requirements. These taxes may relate to property located within the state, payroll, business licenses, industry-related taxes, taxes on special types of businesses, goods, services, gross receipts, and net worth taxes. State and city taxes can typically be deducted from the federal income tax.

Tax planning is the main part of business operations, essential for business success. Thus, business owners should consult qualified professionals to manage the complex requirements of the U.S. tax system. Almost all businesses hire an accountant experienced in state and federal tax issues and payroll matters to supervise the business operations and be sure they are in compliance with the extensive and ever-changing tax requirements.

Most companies also retain the services of a tax attorney. Tax attorneys do not prepare and file tax returns and other tax-related forms, but they structure, plan, and advise on business and individual tax matters, specific items on the returns, and disclosure issues. While some companies do not need the assistance of a tax attorney on a regular basis, tax attorney services are necessary during the important events in a company's business life, such as the start-up phase, major transactions, acquisitions of assets, mergers, restructurings, and liquidation. Communications with tax attorneys are protected by the attorney/client privilege.

CHAPTER 8

Banking in the United States

The U.S. banking system is the largest and most diversified in the world. Both national and international banks are present in the U.S. market. Commercial banks, investment banks, savings banks, savings and loan associations, credit unions, leasing companies, finance companies, and factoring companies that provide asset-based financing are some examples of the different types of financial institutions that comprise the U.S. banking system. They offer the widest range of products and services globally, ranging from personal to small business, corporate, and institutional banking and can tailor their services to the specific needs of a client.

When an entrepreneur starts a new business or contemplates business operations, the relationship with a bank is of prime concern. For a new business entity or a branch of the existing one, the first step should be to open a basic checking account. The checking account is used to conduct daily business operations, such as paying to the vendors, accepting transactions from the customers, paying employees, and making other regular business expenses. Nowadays, more and more transactions are done electronically; online banking allows owners to access their accounts and complete necessary transactions from anywhere, twenty-four/seven.

A company may also require a merchant account, which is necessary in order to accept payments from customers by credit or debit card. This convenience may draw more clients to the business, as well as allow existing clients to pay their bills more quickly and conveniently, since they do not have to pay cash out of pocket.

If the business earns profits that it does not need to spend or otherwise distribute immediately, those profits may be deposited into a savings account. The company will thereby generate interest. These accounts may be free to utilize if a business maintains a certain minimum balance and can be used to set aside a portion of excess liquid assets while earning interest. Money held in a U.S. bank account is insured by the federal government up to $250,000.

In addition to savings and checking accounts, most banks provide other useful services to their customers, including cash management and payroll services.

Cash management service means that the bank's employees, not the company's, will process the payments, manage cash balances, retrieve all necessary information on the accounts, and notify the owners of any upcoming payments so they can plan for their expenses accordingly. This service helps to effectively manage company money without taking time from the core business dealings. Being able to delegate these duties to the bank instead of their staff allows business owners to use their human resources in a more productive way.

Payroll service allows companies to outsource all their payroll matters to the bank. It will make payments to the employees from the business checking account, prepare and file payroll statements with the government agencies, and submit the reports to the company management.

Borrowing in the U.S.

Commercial banks supply the most funds to businesses. Entrepreneurs may need to do certain purchases for their businesses on credit and use available cash for other purposes, or they may decide to invest in equipment or real estate but do not have enough personal assets for such a sizeable purchase. In such cases, various types of financing are available.

Short-term Financing: This is usually arranged as a line of credit. It is an easily accessible source of funds for everyday working capital needs. Entrepreneurs pay via credit card, then make periodic payments to the bank until the card balance is satisfied in full. Credit card interest charges are tax deductible.

Middle-Term Loans: These loans are generally issued by a bank for a term of five to seven years. As a condition of the loan, a bank usually requires execution of a note and a formal loan agreement that may contain covenants restricting the borrower's decision-making regarding certain big transactions. The bank may also require personal guarantees of the business owners, audited financial statements of the company, and even some sort of collateral if a company does not have an established good credit history.

Long-Term Loans: This type of loan exists to help companies purchase capital goods or consolidate their business debts so they will only have to deal with one creditor as opposed to multiple ones. Real estate and equipment financing often involve long-term loans, and these loans may be issued for fifteen- or thirty-year terms.

Leasing: Another way to make sizeable purchases is to lease with an option to buy at the end of the lease term. Leasing is often used to finance the purchase of expensive personal property and equipment. A bank or a leasing company will purchase equipment for the entrepreneur, then lease it to the entrepreneur for a specified periodic payment. The leasing company retains actual title to the equipment. The lessee could treat the rental payments as a current expense on his or her financial statements, thus reducing net taxable income. At the end of the lease term, the lessee usually has an option to return the equipment or to buy it at a depreciated price.

A wide variety of federal, state, and locally sponsored incentives are available for new and expanding businesses, depending on the size and scope of the proposed project and its location. These incentives may include loans with reduced rates, grants, tax credits, tax abatements, and others.

Other Banking Matters

Most U.S. banks operate under a know-your-customer policy that requires them to verify true existence and good faith of a business and its financial transactions and the identity of the persons who have signature authority on the accounts and allows them to request additional documents of the company in case some issues arise.

Informational returns may sometimes be required on the transfer of substantial amounts of cash. Banks will notify the IRS about any cash transactions in the amount of $10,000 or more.

Any U.S. individual or company who has a financial interest in or signature authority over any financial account in a foreign country, where the aggregate value of these accounts exceeds $10,000 at any time during the calendar year, is required to file a Report of Foreign Banks and Financial Accounts with the IRS by June 30 of the following year. Failure to meet this filing requirement could result in high civil and criminal penalties.

In addition to the basic banking services of treasury, lending, payments, and cash management, certain banks provide tailored, sophisticated banking solutions in the areas of corporate finance, corporate investment, leasing, structured finance, commercial finance (factoring), real estate finance, insurance, and equity and debt capital markets. Banks in the USA assist businesses with growing, managing their day-to-day banking needs, and providing a full range of banking services to help entrepreneurs achieve their business goals.

CHAPTER 9

U.S. Capital Markets

Financing in the United States can take different forms, some of which we've already mentioned. The most common are personal assets, private loans, commercial bank borrowings and equity or debt offerings. Personal assets are limited. Not everyone has connections to private loans from high-networth individuals or wealthy friends and relatives. Commercial bank borrowings may not satisfy all financial needs for several reasons: They are difficult or impossible to obtain for some companies (especially start-ups), they require high annual interest rates for payback, and only a limited amount is available. Therefore, companies may choose to seek capital in public markets or private transactions by offering participation in the company's future profits to proposed investors.

The laws governing private or public offerings of company interests, known as securities offerings, are extensive and require strict compliance, including registration with various regulatory organizations. Securities transactions are subject to regulations under both federal and state laws.

All securities offerings in the United States must either be registered with the Securities and Exchange Commission (SEC) or completed in compliance with an exemption from the registration requirements and applicable state securities laws. Failure to comply with these requirements exposes the issuer and its officers and directors to potential civil and criminal liability.

Because of the cost and time required to complete a registered public offering of securities, many securities offerings are completed as private placements, pursuant to an exemption from registration. Private placement is an offering of securities for sale to a limited number of sophisticated investors. Several exemptions are available, but it is essential that the issuer consult with an attorney who specializes in securities matters before offering or selling securities in the United States.

In addition to satisfying the registration requirements, issuers planning to offer securities in the United States must also comply with the disclosure and anti-fraud provisions of the federal and state securities laws. In general, these laws impose liability both for misstatements and omissions of material facts in connection with a securities offering. The liability extends to the issuer, its officers, directors, and other involved parties.

Companies that complete a registered public offering of securities or that list shares for sale in the United States are subject to the periodic reporting requirements of the federal securities laws.

State securities laws, commonly known as "blue sky" laws, coexist and regulate various securities transactions simultaneously with the federal laws. Although states continue to seek greater uniformity in these blue sky laws, state security laws are still characterized by great diversity of language and interpretation. It is very important to know precisely applicable state laws before taking any action in relation to securities.

The facilities through which securities are traded are known as markets. The biggest American securities markets—the New York Stock Exchange, the American Stock Exchange, and NASDAQ—have their own rules and regulations concerning operating and listing standards. If a company or any other market participant wants to work through these markets, they must confirm the current requirements and abide by them.

While laws differ from state to state, the federal securities law basically consists of eight statutes that are periodically amended.

- Securities Act of 1933

- Securities Exchange Act of 1934

- Trust Indenture Act of 1939

- Investment Company Act of 1940

- Investment Advisers Act of 1940

- Securities Investor Protection Act of 1970 (SIPA)

- Sarbanes-Oxley Act of 2002

- Dodd-Frank Wall Street Reform and Consumer Protection Act of 2010

- Rules and Regulations

Securities Act of 1933

This Act regulates initial public offerings of securities. It has two basic provisions:

- prohibits offers and sales of securities that are not registered with SEC to ensure that investors receive financial and other significant information concerning securities being offered for sale, and

- prohibits deceit, misrepresentations, and other fraudulent practices in any offer or sale of securities.

Not all offerings of securities must be registered with the SEC. The SEC exempts certain securities offerings from the registration process in order to alleviate the financial and administrative burden for the companies that make a small offering, with a minimal risk of hurting the general public. Some exemptions from the registration requirement include:

- private offerings to a limited number of persons or institutions;

- offerings of limited size;

- intrastate offerings; and

- securities of municipal, state, and federal governments.

Securities Exchange Act of 1934

This Act regulates trading in securities that are already issued and outstanding (secondary markets). It is much more extensive than its predecessor in 1933 and contains a number of distinct groups of provisions aimed at different participants in the securities trading process. The 1934 Act:

• authorizes SEC to administer the 1933 Act;

• imposes disclosure and other numerous requirements on publicly held companies;

• regulates proxy solicitations, tender offers, and insider trading;

• prohibits various manipulative or deceptive practices in connection with the purchase or sale of securities;

• restricts the amount of credit that may be extended for the purchase of securities;

• requires brokers and dealers to register with the SEC and regulates their activities; and

• empowers SEC with broad authority over all aspects of securities industry, including registration, regulation, and supervision of national securities exchanges and associations, clearing agencies, transfer agents, and securities information processors.

Trust Indenture Act of 1939

This Act applies to debt securities such as bonds, debentures, and notes in excess of a specified amount, offered for public sale. Even though such securities may be registered under the 1933 Act, they must also be qualified under this Act, which imposes the standards of independence and responsibility on the indenture trustees and requires other provisions to be included in the indenture for the protection of the investors.

Investment Company Act of 1940

This Act regulates publicly owned companies that are primarily engaged in the business of investing and trading in securities. It regulates their organization, management, capital structure, contracts, and policy and requires companies to disclose their financial conditions and investment policies to the investors on a regular basis with the purpose to avoid the conflict of interest and to enable the investors to make informed decisions knowing the company's structure, investment objectives, and other material information.

Investment Advisers Act of 1940

This 1940 Act regulates the registration and business activity of investment advisers (individuals and firms compensated for advising others about securities investments) who have more than $100 million of assets under management or advise a registered investment company. Advisers with less than $100 million of assets under management are regulated by their home state laws.

Securities Investor Protection Act (SIPA) of 1970

SIPA supervises the liquidation of securities firms that are suffering financial difficulties and directs the payment of claims asserted by their clients.

Sarbanes-Oxley Act of 2002

The Act makes extensive reforms to corporate governance and disclosure requirements for public companies. It adopted a number of corporate governance regulations to enhance corporate responsibility and financial disclosures. It also increased accountability of corporate officers, attorneys, and accountants, combats corporate and accounting fraud and imposes increased criminal penalties for violations of securities laws.

Dodd-Frank Wall Street Reform and Consumer Protection Act of 2010

This legislation set out to reshape the U.S. regulatory system in a number of areas, including but not limited to consumer protection, trading restrictions, credit ratings, regulation of financial products, corporate governance, disclosure, and transparency.

Other Securities Rules and Regulations

In addition to the above federal statutes, various agencies have authority to issue their own rules and regulations, which are mandatory to follow for the securities markets participants. The SEC has broad rule-making powers, and it exercises these by prescribing different kinds of regulations, issuing forms, reports, and engaging in informal rule-making, such as the publication of releases, no-action letters, and statements that demonstrate the view of the agency in a particular matter. Self-regulatory organizations such as stock exchanges regulate the activities of their members, in addition to federal and state agencies. If an individual or a firm is using facilities of a self-regulated organization, they should comply with certain rules and requirements issued by that organization. Also, court and administrative decisions present a comprehensive body of law and interpret the application of current federal statutes. The combination of all these rules governs all securities-related activities, and it is important to know which are applicable to the transaction or market participant at hand.

CHAPTER 10

Internet Business

In today's technology-driven world, more and more online businesses are established every day. It is predicted that in the very near future, even fewer people will be attached to the physical locations of their offices or stores. The Internet allows great flexibility; less start-up and operational costs; much wider outreach to markets, consumers and professionals for assistance; and availability of many other useful business resources (e.g. the use of forum sites, professional sites, and targeted advertising). Establishing an online business presence can be a lucrative way to sell, buy, market, advertise, and otherwise promote goods or services.

From a legal perspective, the same laws and regulations apply to online and offline businesses. When starting an online business, entrepreneurs should be aware of the laws, rules, and regulations that apply to their industry in general and what specific legal considerations must be given to their type of venture (contractual relationships, employment matters, form of business organization, intellectual property issues, and so on).

In addition to the legal matters that all businesses face, online businesses must comply with special laws and regulations that govern commercial activities in cyberspace. Also, the owners of online businesses should review how such general laws as, for example, intellectual property, contracts law, taxation, and customer protection law are interpreted, applied, and operate in cyberspace, since the specifics of online presence impose certain questions and practical rules.

Online commercial activities are regulated simultaneously by federal, state, and local (municipal) laws. The major federal laws that guide online business are: The Anti-Cybersquatting Consumer Protection Act of 1999; Selling on the Internet: Prompt Delivery Rules; and the Children's Online Privacy Protection Act.

The Federal Trade Commission (FTC) is the primary federal agency that regulates ecommerce activities, digital rights, commercial use of email, online advertising, and consumer privacy. There is an extensive list of FTC ecommerce rules and regulations, and all entrepreneurs with an online presence should be familiar with those that apply to their type of business.

Taxes

Online businesses are required to pay the same federal taxes as regular businesses. There is a question, however, about state and local taxes; whether online business is responsible for payment of state and local taxes is very fact specific. The general rule about state and local sales taxes (whether an online company has to collect those taxes from its customers and pay them to state and local revenue agencies) is that if an on-line business has some physical location with a state (such as a storefront, office, or warehouse), it should charge its customers the sales tax rate required by the jurisdiction where that business is located. If the company does not have a presence in a particular state, it is not required to collect sales taxes from the customers. Simply put, online retailers who do not have a physical presence in any state and supply goods or services by mail or email to customers/clients in various locations cannot possibly comply with all the tax jurisdictions within the United States, over 7,500 of them at the time this book was written. Forcing businesses to collect such diverse and sizeable sales taxes would put a strain on interstate commerce

International Business

If the company does business internationally, its owners should be familiar and comply with international trade and contract law, shipping, tax, customs regulations, and other considerations, depending on particular countries where they intend to conduct commercial activities.

Intellectual Property

We have already spent a great deal of time discussing intellectual property (IP), but it has become a growing concern with the development of online businesses. Because the Internet allows easier access to company information, it is possible to inadvertently infringe upon someone's intellectual property (IP) rights or become a victim of bad business practices yourself. It may be difficult to maintain the thin line between healthy competition and adoption of the successful business practices and copying protected information. Online business owners are mainly concerned about protecting their domain names, trademarks, copyrighted items, patents, and licenses, all of which fall under U.S. Intellectual Property Law and are to benefit from the same protection as offline matters. With the rapid development of the Internet and the unique possibilities it offers to users on a global scale, there are certain specifics regarding the exploitation and infringement of IP rights online.

The 1998 U.S. Digital Millennium Copyright Act (DMCA) was adopted to reflect those differences and clarify IP law in relation to online practices. It protects digital works, including text, movies, music, art, other forms of electronic information, and data published online. The Act contains many provisions explaining how an IP proprietor can protect his or her rights and avoid the infringement of the IP rights of others.

A common problem is when someone obtains copyrighted material via the Internet and uses it without permission, hoping such acts will go undetected in such a wide online Net. Pursuant to the DMCA, the IP owner is entitled to the same various damages as would be claimed in the real world and has a right to prevent others from using materials without obtaining necessary licenses from the owner. Copyright infringement can have severe consequences, including criminal penalties and potentially substantial civil damages for each infringement, in addition to bearing the legal fees of the copyright owner, if that owner prevails in court.

DMCA also explains what measures a website owner can take to prevent infringement of others' IP rights. If he or she uses another's materials to promote the public interest, such as education, scholarship, criticism, parody, uses a relatively small amount of the total copyrighted work and not for profit, these actions may fall under the fair use doctrine, and infringement charges may be avoided. If someone intends to use IP work under the fair use doctrine, the best practice is to give credit to the original author or the source from which the material was obtained. This will avoid confusion regarding the legal ownership of the intellectual property.

Terms of Use of the Website

The information posted on a website may result in a binding contract. Puffery or advertisement may become an enforceable contract, as was earlier noted. Thus, it is critically important to post your Terms of Use on your company website. These should be fully compatible with the business of the company, reflect owner's intentions and goals, limit the liability, express other information, which may be necessary for the site visitors to know, and otherwise comply with the applicable U.S. law and regulations. Terms of Use posted on the website is considered to be a contract between the site owner and its visitors, even if it is not named this way. It prevents site visitors from claiming misunderstanding, inducement, or any other form of misleading. The Terms of Use will generally include many disclaimers.

All activities that are illegal in real life are also illegal online. In addition, Cyber Law defines what actions are illegal online, pertaining to those that are nonexistent in the offline world. Examples include child pornography, cyber stalking, online fraud, cyber scams, hacking, cyber harassment, and virus attacks. The objective of Cyber Law is to protect Internet users and make the Internet a safe place for business and personal interactions. Cyber Law is enforced by courts and police officers across the country. If a person violates Cyber Law he or she can be subject to civil and criminal liabilities, ranging from fines and penalties to jail time. Cyber Law is also monitored and enforced by the United States Federal Bureau of Investigation (FBI).

CHAPTER 11

Selling Goods in the USA

If the business of the company is selling goods in the United States, its commercial activities are governed by both common contractual law and the Uniform Commercial Code (UCC), a set of laws relating to commercial transactions. The UCC modernizes contract law and allows certain exceptions from the common law in contracts between merchants. It has been promulgated in an effort to facilitate the contract formation between the market participants and to harmonize the law of sales and other commercial transactions in all fifty states within the United States of America. At this point in time, nearly all states have adopted it.

The UCC is divided into nine articles, each containing provisions that relate to a specific area of commercial law. Article 2 governs the sale of tangible, movable goods, not services, real estate, or intangible property, such as trademarks, patents, and copyrights. Those are governed by common contractual law.

If the contract for goods is at issue and the provision between common law and the UCC is in conflict, the UCC prevails. Also, if the parties have not addressed the particular term in their agreement, the UCC default provisions will fill the gaps in such transactions. If the company is actively involved in the sale of goods, managers and other employees with the decision-making power should be familiar with the main provisions of the UCC Article 2.

Selling goods creates a bilateral contractual relationship between a seller and a purchaser. All contracts for sale involve a common concept: the delivery of goods in exchange for payment of money. However, the legal procedures of doing so, as well as the recourses available under Article 2 of the UCC, are different from the provisions of general contracts law. It is beneficial to know the major differences.

Under the common law, the offer can be revoked before accepted with certain exceptions (option contracts, foreseeable reliance, start of the performance by the other party are among such exceptions). Article 2 of the UCC provides that if a merchant (almost every businessperson is a merchant under its broad definition) promises in a signed, written document to keep an offer open for a certain period of time, he or she cannot revoke the offer before the promised period ends. This firm offer can be irrevocable only for three months, subject to extension thereafter.

Under the common law, the acceptance of the offer must mirror the offer. The other party must respond "yes" or "no." Adding or changing any terms operates as a rejection of the offer. Under Article 2, acceptance does not have to mirror the offer. The underlying policy is to facilitate contract formation between businesspeople. However, changes or additions made by the other party become the terms of the contract only if both negotiating parties are merchants, the term is not a material change, and there is no objection received within a reasonable time. If the added term is customary in the industry, it is not considered material (e.g., certain delivery requirements). If a newly added term imposes additional obligations on the other party or alters the subject matter of the transaction, it is a material change. In the latter case, the acceptance of the offer is still valid, but those additional terms will not be included in the final contract. The offering party can, however, keep out even a minor change if it objects to it within a reasonable time.

Under the common law, if the major contractual provisions are not performed as agreed, there is a breach. Article 2 says there is no breach if the seller sends other goods as an accommodation to the buyer. If the seller sends the wrong goods, it is a breach of the contract, but if the seller includes a note saying, "I'm out of that product, but I'm sending you this in the hope that it may meet your needs," there is no automatic breach. The buyer does not have to keep the unsatisfactory goods. Rather, the buyer has two options: cancel the contract or require the seller to ship the proper goods and separately negotiate any damages caused by the delay.

Under the common law, if there is a need to modify a contract, the modification will be valid only if the parties received additional consideration for doing so (consideration is something bargained for, such as additional compensation, savings, non-material value). In sale-of-goods transactions under Article 2, new consideration is not required to modify an already existing contract. The parties only have to show good faith in proceeding with it. As an example, parties can agree to raise the price of the contract if it is reasonable. In such a case, the buyer does not receive additional consideration; actually, he or she may pay more, but this modification will be valid if there is a good faith reason for it.

Under the common law, the contract can be formed either orally or in writing. Article 2 and the Statute of Frauds require that the contract to be in writing in order to be valid if the sale of goods is for $500 or more.

Under the common law. the contract must contain all material terms to be enforceable (who, what, when, where, how much). In the sale-of-goods contracts under Article 2, the contract is enforceable if it has a quantity term and is signed by the party to be charged with in case of breach (the prospective defendant). The following note would be enforceable contract under Article 2: "I agree to buy fifty widgets from A&A Corp., signed, John Doe." In some situations, the seller can use his or her own signed writing to satisfy the Article 2 requirement. This is known as "merchant's confirmatory memo". Such writing qualifies if:

- both parties are merchants;

- the writing claims a prior oral agreement;

- the writing is signed and has a quantity stated; and

- no written objection is received from a buyer within ten days.

Who bears the risk of loss while goods are in transit? This is a major concern for both parties. The parties can negotiate the allocation of the risk in the contract. If the goods are transported by a common carrier such as UPS or FedEx, the risk of loss shifts to the buyer when the seller completes its delivery obligations. The seller's delivery obligations are subject to negotiation between the parties. The commonly used term in contracts is free on board (FOB), followed by the name of a place. If the FOB is followed by the seller's city, it means the seller must make delivery arrangements with a common carrier and notify the buyer. From that moment, the risk of loss is on the buyer, even while the goods are in transit. If FOB refers to some other place, the seller must deliver the goods to that specific place (usually where the buyer is located, unless otherwise agreed), and only upon delivery does the risk of loss flows to the buyer.

In non-carrier cases, when a buyer has to pick up or a seller has to deliver the goods, if a seller is a merchant, under Article 2, the seller bears the risk of loss until the buyer takes possession of the goods. If a seller is not a merchant, the seller bears the risk of loss until it makes the goods available to a buyer by notifying the buyer where and when to pick them up.

Under the common law, a contract is satisfied if it is substantially performed; even if the performance is not perfect, no material breach happened. Under Article 2 of the UCC, if the delivered goods are not perfect, the buyer may reject the goods under the perfect tender rule. The seller has an option to cure before he or she is officially in breach, provided the time for performance has not expired.

If the buyer keeps goods without objection after having a reasonable opportunity to inspect, the buyer is considered to have accepted the goods, but the buyer can still claim damages for any shortcomings. If the buyer rejects the goods, he or she is entitled to the following recourses:

- return the goods to the seller at the seller's expense;

- get a refund on any money paid for the goods; and

- receive damages from the seller for breach of contract.

The seller usually cannot reclaim the goods from a non-paying buyer. The two exceptions to this rule are:

1. A buyer was insolvent when he or she received the goods and the seller makes a demand within ten days after the buyer received the goods.

2. A buyer misrepresented its solvency in writing within three months before delivery, then the seller can reclaim the goods at any time.

Otherwise, if the buyer does not properly pay for the goods received, the seller's only option is to sue for damages.

Warranties

Article 2 of the UCC also governs warranties arising in connection with the sale of goods. Under the UCC, there are two types of warranties, express and implied.

Express Warranty: This is created by any promise, statement of fact, description of the goods, demonstration of the sample, or affirmation made by the seller. If the seller states expressly that the goods have certain qualities and they do not, the buyer can sue the seller for breach of warranty. A mere opinion is not a warranty: "These goods are top quality."

Implied Warranties: The seller is deemed to have made certain implied warranties of merchantability even if he or she remains silent about the quality of a product. The mere act of selling the product produces an implied warranty. By selling certain goods, the seller represents that the goods are of a quality normally acceptable in the particular trade and fit for their ordinary purpose. To be liable for implied warranties, however, the seller must be a merchant who regularly deals in the kind of goods at issue and has specialized knowledge about those goods. For example, when a shoe wholesaler sells shoes, he or she makes implied warranties regarding the quality of the shoes, since he deals with this kind of goods on regular basis. However, if the same shoe wholesaler sells his or her office equipment, he or she cannot be held liable for implied warranties since it is not the nature of his or her business to sell office equipment; he or she does it as an occasional sale. In the event that goods do not conform to the implied warranty, the buyer is entitled to recover the same damages as would be available in the case of an express warranty.

The seller can disclaim implied but not express warranties. For example, when the contract says "as-is" or "with all faults" and there is no other statement about quality, the implied warranties are disclaimed. However, if the seller made some express warranties about the goods and then wrote in the contract, "All warranties are disclaimed," the express warranties will survive this disclaimer.

Article 2 of the UCC contains detailed extensive rules governing the transactions involving the sale of goods. Some of these rules may or may not be applicable to different types of deals and relationships between the parties. The information provided herein is a brief guidance of the basic, general terms that are applicable in all sale-of-goods contracts. Each separate transaction may contain some specifics, or certain facts may be present during the negotiation or execution process that must be carefully considered and evaluated before the parties commence their commercial dealings.

CHAPTER 12

Importing Goods to the USA

Selling imported goods within the United States can be a very profitable business venture. There is always high demand for new or improved products in any category, from food to furniture. There is a great number of different national communities in the U.S., and those nationals often crave goods from their countries of origin and are willing to pay lucrative premiums for them. The American market is famous for free trade and vast opportunities, giving entrepreneurs the chance to offer something unique to the customers.

The U.S. import laws are designed to facilitate the importation process. U.S. Customs quotes are some of the lowest in the world (the average is 3 percent), an importer is not required to have a license or permit to engage in such business (other agencies may require a permit, license, or other certification, depending on the products to be imported; will be discussed below), and the U.S. has entered into special trade agreements with different countries to further promote international trade and business relationships.

The U.S. Customs and Border Protection of the Department of Homeland Security (CBP), along with a number of other government agencies, regulate goods imported into the United States. The U.S. Customs territory includes fifty states, the District of Columbia, and Puerto Rico. There are over 325 ports of entry located throughout the United States including seaports, airports, and land border crossings.

When contemplating the import of certain merchandise, first and foremost, entrepreneurs must find out whether those products can be lawfully imported into the USA. Then, they should familiarize themselves with applicable legal requirements of the U.S. Customs and Import Laws, whether licenses and permits are required to import and sell those products, and how to prepare the import documentation so it complies with the U.S. law (there is a U.S. legislation relating to particular types of products, what they can and cannot contain, their labeling, etc.).

Business owners need to have complete information regarding importation procedures in order to calculate the expenses, time consumption, and overall profitability of the venture. Moreover, failure to comply can subject the importer, seller, and other involved parties to fines, penalties, and even seizures of the goods.

With few exceptions, all merchandise coming into the United States must be declared with the Bureau of Customs and Border Protection, must clear Customs, and an importer must pay a Customs duty unless the goods are specifically exempted from this duty by law before the imported merchandise can be used within the U.S. territory. I will review each step of the importation process in detail below.

Arrival of the Goods

A shipment with the goods arrives at the port of entry. The Customs Service does not notify the interested parties of the arrival of their shipment The importers are responsible for making inquiries themselves about the status of the shipment to ensure that the entry can be filed in a timely manner. Usually, the sender or the carrier of the shipment is asked to notify the receiving party when the goods arrive. Before the declaration of entry and Customs clearance, the goods are held at a bonded warehouse or foreign trade zone.

Goods must be declared for entry into the U.S. within fifteen days of arrival or prior to leaving a bonded warehouse or foreign trade zone. The importer of record is responsible for starting the process of entry and submitting all necessary documentation. The importer of record can be the owner of the goods, the purchaser, or the agent. Customs entry papers may be presented before the merchandise arrives.

Imported goods that were not declared to the CBP in a timely manner are sent to a general order warehouse to be held as unclaimed. The importer is responsible for storage charges during the period the unclaimed merchandise is held at the warehouse. If it remains unclaimed at the end of six months, the merchandise is sold at auction.

Entry of the Goods

Imported goods are considered to legally enter the country when three events occur:

1. a shipment has arrived within the port of entry,

2. delivery of the merchandise has been authorized by CBP, and

3. estimated duties have been paid.

The CBP enforces the completeness and accuracy of import documentation and imposes various penalties for noncompliance, some of which may cause the loss of the entire shipment. Documentation requirements can be extensive in certain cases, but usually the following documents are necessary, referred to as a customs entry package:

• a bill of lading, airway bill, or carrier's certificate;

• a commercial invoice from the seller, which shows the value and description of the merchandise;

• entry manifest (Customs Form 7533) or entry/immediate delivery (Customs Form 3461); and

• packaging lists, certificate of origin, special certificates, if appropriate, and other documents necessary to determine whether the merchandise may be admitted according to the U.S. legal standards.

To facilitate the customs clearance, the CBP and the import community have created the Customs Automated Commercial System (ACS), which receives and processes entry documentation and provides cargo disposition information electronically. Cargo carriers, Customs brokers, and importers may use the system. It reduces clearance time from days to hours or even minutes.

If the imported goods initially arrive to one port of entry and the importer intends to transfer them to another port, for example, the one closer to his or her warehouse or place of distribution, the goods may be sent in-bond from the first port of arrival to another Customs port. Arrangements for in-bond shipments should be made before the goods leave the country of export. The importer of record is not required to file the entry package, pay the duties and processing fees, or deal with other Customs formalities until the goods arrive at the port of final destination.

When the entry is filed, the importer indicates the tariff classification and pays any estimated duty and processing fee if not exempt by law. Posting of a surety bond containing various provisions, including an obligation to pay any increased duty that may be later found to be due, may also be required.

Duty Rates

The United States imposes tariffs or Customs duties on the imports of goods. The duty is levied at the time of import and is paid by the importer of record before he or she can withdraw the goods from the Customs. Customs duties vary, depending on product classification, country of origin, and valuation.

Classification: All imported goods are categorized according to the Harmonized Tariff Schedule of the United States (HTSUS), issued by the International Trade Commission. Classification refers to how the imported goods are described in HTSUS (e.g. vegetables, textiles, auto parts) and will determine the duty rate, admissibility into the U.S., anti-dumping duties, and whether the product is eligible for special duty quotas. Classification determination is a complicated process and may require a significant amount of information related to the imported goods. HTSUS does not always describe the goods in the same manner as they are described at their countries of origin. The importer is responsible for properly classifying merchandise according to the HTSUS standards before entry to the U.S.

Country of Origin: Rates of tax on transaction values vary by country of origin. Importers are required to make accurate declarations as to the country of origin for all merchandise. Sometimes the country of origin is easily determined, but it can be more complicated in others. For example, when the parts of the products were manufactured in one country and assembled in another, U.S. Customs will apply the higher rate between the two countries of origin, unless the work done on the product and other connections to that country were minimal.

All foreign goods must be individually marked to indicate country of origin, though a limited number of goods is exempt from this requirement. This mark on the product must be made in such way that the ultimate consumer of the product will clearly understand the product's country of origin.

Goods from Canada, Mexico, Israel, some Third World countries, and certain other countries may be eligible for reduced duties. Most countries qualify for normal duties as a most favored nation. Goods from countries not considered most favored nations are subject to increased duties.

It bears mentioning that the North American Free Trade Agreement (NAFTA) was adopted in 1994 by the governments of the U.S., Canada, and Mexico. It eliminates tariffs on most goods originating in these member countries.

Valuation: U.S. regulations for valuing imported goods implement the WTO Valuation Agreement. The dutiable value of merchandise is determined by Customs. Generally, the transaction value of the merchandise serves as the basis of appraisement. Transaction value is the price the buyer actually pays to the seller for the goods being imported. The rate of duty that the CBP assesses on a particular shipment of imported goods is not binding for future shipments of the same or similar merchandise. Where there is uncertainty, the CBP has a binding ruling program, whereby importers can request a written ruling as to the proper classification and applicable rates of duty.

NAFTA was mentioned earlier in relation to goods from Canada and Mexico, but goods from many other countries may be exempt from duty under the trade agreements between those countries and the United States. Certain types of goods are exempt from duty, regardless of the source. Even if the imported goods are exempt from Customs duty, they must still be declared and examined for compliance with other laws (product specifications, safety, labeling, etc.).

When goods are not exempt from duties, they are properly classified and appraised according to U.S. valuation procedures. After that, various methods of duty calculations may be applied. Most often, *ad valorem* rates are used, which are calculated as a percentage of the value of the goods (such as 4 percent). Some articles, however, are dutiable at a specific rate of duty that applies different quotas to a piece, gallon, pound, and other measures. Others are charged at a compound rate of duty, a combination of both *ad valorem* and specific rates.

After duties have been paid, the CBP approves the goods for import. They can then be removed from the port of entry, bonded warehouse, or free-trade zone.

If the duty has been paid on the particular goods and an importer then exports those goods to another country without doing substantial modifications to them, the importer can seek a refund of duties. The process of claiming a refund is known as duty drawback.

Status of Entry

Duties do not have to be paid if the goods are not to be used or distributed on the territory of the United States but are held in a bond warehouse or free-trade zone. The importer of record has to pay storage fees to the warehouse owner nevertheless.

Foreign-trade zones are areas physically located in the United States but legally outside the Customs territory of the United States. Such zones are generally near ports of entry and are limited in scope and operation based on approval of the Foreign-Trade Zones Board. Goods in a forcign-trade zone are not considered imported to the United States until they leave that zone. Foreign goods may be used to manufacture other goods within the zone for further export without payment of Customs duties or holding the merchandise in such zones can postpone the duty payments and custom formalities until the importer actually needs those goods for business. Goods may be stored in a bonded warehouse or a foreign-trade zone in the United States for up to five years without payment of duties.

Restricted Merchandise

Many exported and imported products are regulated by federal agencies. These include but are not limited to:

- Alcoholic beverages

- Animals and animal products

- Certain drugs and pharmaceuticals

- Firearms and ammunition

- Fruits and nuts

- Meat and meat products

- Milk, dairy, and cheese products

- Plants and plant products

- Poultry and poultry products

- Trademarked articles

- Vegetables

Certain items in these categories may be prohibited for import at all.

If a company exports or imports these regulated types of products, it may be required to register with special U.S. governmental agencies that supervise commercial activities and compliance in that particular industry (e.g. U.S. Food and Drug Administration for food and beverage products), to appoint a U.S. representative, to file certain documents with regard to each shipment, and to retain records for the prescribed period of time. Also, it may be required to obtain specific licenses and permits from the responsible agency. Most of the above items are regulated by the Bureau of Alcohol, Tobacco, and Firearms, Animal and Plant Health Inspection Service, Agricultural Marketing Service, U.S. Fish and Wildlife Service, and the Food and Drug Administration.

Prohibited Merchandise

The regulations administered by the Office of Foreign Assets Control (FAC) generally prohibit the unlicensed importation of merchandise, except information and informational materials, of Cuban, Iranian, Iraqi, Libyan, or North Korean origin. Goods may not be imported from or through commercial entities owned or controlled by the governments or private citizens of Cuba, Iran, Iraq, Libya, or North Korea, regardless of the location of the entity. Vessels or aircraft under the registry, ownership, or control of the governments of or commercial entities in the above areas may not import merchandise into the United States.

Customs Brokers

Many entrepreneurs who are in the business of importing goods into the U.S. choose to retain the services of a Customs broker to help them through the process of Customs clearance. Customs brokers are licensed by the U.S. Department of the Treasury, and their primary service is to represent the importer in filing and processing the Customs entry with the CBP. They may also provide guidance with tariff classification, quota compliance, and anticipation of difficulties in the entry of products.

Customs Examination of Goods and Documents

Examination of goods and documents is necessary to determine the compliance with the U.S. laws and regulations and the correctness of the submitted information. During the examination, the representatives of the CBP review:

• the value of the goods for customs purposes and their dutiable status;

• the appropriate marking and labeling of the goods (U.S. law has special requirement to the labeling of different types of goods, which must be known and satisfied by the importer in order to sell the goods in the U.S.);

• whether the goods have been correctly invoiced (the U.S. law in general and anti-dumping law particularly require arm's-length dealings between the parties to the transaction, meaning that one party cannot sell the goods to another at intentionally much lower price than it sells the same goods to others);

• whether the shipment contains prohibited articles;

• whether requirements of other federal agencies have been met, if applicable; and

• whether goods in excess of the invoiced quantities are present or a shortage of goods exists.

When examination or appraisal of the goods by Customs reveals differences from the entered descriptions by the importer, or when the Customs finds that a different rate of duty than the one indicated by the importer applies, an increase in duties may be assessed.

When all the information has been acquired, including the report of the Customs import specialist as to the Customs value of the goods and the laboratory report, if required, a final determination of the applicable duty is made. This is known as *liquidation* of the entry. At this time, any overpayment of the duty is returned or underpayments billed.

Protest

If an importer disagrees with the CBP valuation of the goods, the imposed duties, or other conclusions of Customs, he or she may, within ninety days after the date of liquidation or other decision, protest the decision and request an administrative review. Notice of the denial or acceptance of a protest, in whole or in part, will be mailed to the importer or to his or her agent. If the importer's protest has been denied, the importer may then litigate the agency decision. If an importer wishes judicial review, he or she will be required to file a summons in the Court of International Trade.

Mail Shipments

A formal entry is required for any commercial mail shipment exceeding $2,000 in value. Formal entry is also required, regardless of value, for commercial shipments of textiles from all countries and all made-to-measure suits from Hong Kong. The parcel is forwarded to the Customs office nearest the addressee. Customs notifies the addressee of the parcel's arrival and the location of the Customs office where Customs formalities may be arranged. Customs clearance will require filing an entry in the same manner as for shipments arriving by vessel or airfreight.

Penalties

Certain civil and criminal penalties apply for failures to follow CBP rules and pay duty. The penalties may be as high as twice the value of the goods, plus twenty years in jail for certain intentional offenses. In addition, goods of persons subject to such penalties may be seized and sold by the CBP at auction.

Antidumping Law

Another area of law that an importer must know about is the U.S. Antidumping law. Dumping is an unfair trade practice, when a business sells goods in the United States at a price lower than what it charges for a comparable product in another market or when the company sells its goods at a price below the cost of production for those goods and the imports cause material injury or threat of material injury to a U.S. industry. Sometimes a seller engages in such practice intentionally to expand market share and reduce competition. Big companies may afford to sustain temporary losses in order to gain bigger profits later. Dumping also can occur inadvertently due to a seller's lack of awareness of the way the law defines what activities are considered dumping. The U.S. Department of Commerce (DOC) conducts antidumping investigations when suspicions arise. To determine whether or not a company is dumping the U.S. market, the DOC compares the prices and costs to produce similar products in the countries that are economically and otherwise comparable to the one where the goods were made and calculates an actual cost of production. It then compares the prices of the goods at issue with the average sale prices in the comparable countries, as well as in the country where the goods are coming from. If the goods are imported in the U.S. at the much lower rates, the dumping may be taking place.

Antidumping laws are strictly enforced in the United States. If the DOC finds that dumping has occurred and the U.S. International Trade Commission (ITC) finds that the imports have caused material injury or threat of material injury to a U.S. industry, the DOC will issue an antidumping order, imposing additional duties on goods subject to that order. Antidumping orders can stay in place for five to thirty years.

Defending oneself in an antidumping investigation can be costly and time consuming. Moreover, because the U.S. government will typically require some continued monitoring of a dumping business's activities, the burden and expense may continue for many years. Some general planning and understanding of U.S. antidumping laws can help you avoid these problems.

As was said at the very beginning of this chapter, U.S. import/export laws are designed to promote international trade and market expansion. At the same time, the protection of the consumers and the national economy cannot be compromised. The importation requirements for goods and accompanying documents may be lengthy and complicated, but as in many other types of businesses, once the applicable laws and regulations are studied, the process is thoroughly understood, the accurate initial package of documents is prepared, and the continuous procedures of monitoring and supervision are set in place, the business can be conducted successfully and smoothly, without fear of repercussions for technical errors or lack of information. There are too many good things in the world not to take advantage of them and to limit us just to the products of our country of residence. Let's strive for variety and opportunities to choose!

CHAPTER 13

Consumer Protection

Rights and interests of the consumers are protected on both state and federal levels. There are multiple laws governing various industries to ensure that rights of the consumers, fair trade practices, and competition are duly observed and truthful information is freely disclosed in the marketplace. Federal, state, and local organizations supervise business activities in their respective jurisdictions and review company compliance with the relevant consumer and market protection laws.

The applicability of one or the other regulation depends both on the type of business and the nature of its commercial activities. For example, there are laws that regulate the sale of various goods and services, advertising and marketing, credit issuance and debt collection, privacy and security of consumer information, and many other business interactions. Almost every industry is regulated by consumer protection laws.

These laws are designed to prevent companies from engaging in fraud or deceptive and unfair practices to gain advantage over prospective clients, customers, and competitors. The rationale of protecting not only consumers but other existing companies as well is that the observance of fair business practices and healthy competition is beneficial to the development of marketplace and efficient economy; this, in turn, will benefit the final consumers by delivering the quality products and services at reasonable prices.

Federal consumer protection laws are mainly enforced by the United States Federal Trade Commission (FTC) and the United States Department of Justice. U.S. Congress has granted wide-reaching power to the FTC. The Commission is empowered, among other things, to:

- implement different methods and practices directed at prevention of unfair competition and deceptive acts or practices in commerce;

- sue companies in the court of competent jurisdiction for monetary damages and other relief for conduct that is injurious to consumers;

- issue and enact additional rules and regulations that specify which acts or practices are considered unfair or deceptive and establish requirements and procedures to prevent such acts or practices;

- conduct investigations relating to the organization, business, and management of entities engaged in commerce; and

- make reports and legislative recommendations to the U.S. Congress.

Federal Trade Commission Act (15 U.S.C. §§ 41-58, <u>as</u> <u>amended</u>).

The FTC also has an International Division that strives to promote consumer confidence in the international marketplace by negotiating bilateral consumer protection agreements with other countries and assisting in international litigation.

At the state level, the majority of states have a Department of Consumer Affairs, with functions similar to those of the FTC. State consumer protection agencies parallel FTC activities to ensure that businesses and consumers are well protected within their territories.

Local laws are as important to business owners as federal ones. They can contain more regulations, restrictions, or obligations and provide broad remedies to the consumers for violations, including punitive damages (money used to punish a wrongdoer, as opposed to money used to compensate for harm suffered).

As there are various legal acts that regulate different industries and address many aspects of commercial activities, business owners and managerial personnel should be familiar with the laws applicable to their particular industry. The most popular consumer protection statutes are:

The Consumer Credit Protection Act (CCPA): Also referred to as the Federal Truth in Lending Act, it regulates the credit industry with respect to consumer rights, including credit card companies and credit reporting agencies, as well as loan sharks and wage garnishment.

The Fair Credit Reporting Act (FCRA): The FCRA regulates credit reporting agencies and those who use them.

The Fair Debt Collection Practices Act: This statute prohibits abusive collection practices and gives consumers means to dispute inaccurate debt information.

The Fair Credit Billing Act: This Act deals with billing practices in credit accounts.

The Magnuson-Moss Act of 1973: This Act governs the terms of product warranties for consumer goods, both express and implied.

The Identity Theft and Assumption Deterrence Act: This is meant to address the crimes of identity theft and defines civil and criminal penalties for such wrongdoings.

The Racketeering Influenced and Corrupt Organizations Act (RICO): The RICO Act is designed to attack criminals who try to use legitimate businesses in their illegitimate activities. RICO provides broad civil and criminal remedies if criminal fraud can be alleged and proven. In the case of RICO violations, the award of damages is tripled, the guilty party may be liable for the winning claimant's attorney fees, and there are also forfeiture provisions.

As a result of numerous federal and state legislation and efforts of governmental agencies, U.S. consumers and businesses are much better protected from unfair, deceptive, or anticompetitive practices than in many other jurisdictions. Consumer rights for complete and accurate information and choice are maintained on every level of business dealings, and legitimate businesses are protected from wrongful activities of third parties. The economy can be efficient and well developed only when vigorous competition among product and service providers exists, consumers are supplied with the necessary disclosures that allow them to make educated choices, the offered products and services are high quality, prices are reasonable, and the marketplace is open to new participants.

CHAPTER 14

Product Liability

Companies that manufacture or distribute products in the United States must be conscious of product liability law and its consequences.

Product liability is the area of law in which manufacturers, distributors, suppliers, wholesalers, retailers, and others who make products available to the public are held responsible for the injuries caused by those products. Product liability claims impose strict liability on the responsible parties. Under strict liability doctrine, a merchant is liable if the product is defective, even if the merchant was not negligent in making or providing that product to the customer. Rather than focusing on the misbehavior of a merchant, strict liability claims focus on the product itself. In strict liability terms, when it is shown that the product is defective, a merchant is liable. It is irrelevant whether the manufacturer or supplier exercised great care.

A merchant is anyone who deals with certain products on regular basis. Under the law, not only are manufacturers liable for the defective products, but so are all parties involved in the regular chain of distribution (suppliers, wholesalers, retailers, commercial lessors, etc.). A casual seller, such as someone making random personal sales or selling items on eBay is not a merchant. A service provider is not a merchant as well. Thus, a doctor cannot be held responsible for the broken chair in his office under the product liability doctrine since a doctor is not a merchant of the chairs; rather, the doctor uses them as collateral instruments to his or her services. Commercial lessors, on the other hand, who deal with particular products regularly and when those products constitute the primarily part of their business, are considered to be merchants. A car rental company can be held liable under the product liability theory for the broken cars since dealing with the cars is its primary business and, accordingly, it may be held responsible for the conditions of the provided cars.

Strict liability extends to all parties involved in making a defective product available to the public; i.e. to every person in the distribution chain, not only to the one who deals directly with a prospective plaintiff. A manufacture, wholesaler, retailer, and all other market participants can be sued for the dysfunctional product, depending on their involvement in the distribution of that product. Moreover, such defendants may be liable not only to direct customers and users, but also to any innocent bystanders randomly injured by the defective products.

A product liability claim is a civil lawsuit brought against the maker or distributor of a product, alleging that a person or group of people were injured or damaged by a product that was defective or not suitable for its intended use.

A landmark case in product liability law is *Escola v. Coca-Cola Bottling Company*, 24 Cal. 2d 453 (1944), in which Justice Traynor explained the concept of strict liability with these words: "There is no negligence, however, public policy demands that responsibility be fixed wherever it will most effectively reduce the hazards to life and health inherent in defective products that reach the market. It is evident that the manufacturer can anticipate some hazards and guard against the recurrence of others, as the public cannot... It is to the public interest to discourage the marketing of products having defects that are a menace to the public. If such products nevertheless find their way into the market it is to the public interest to place the responsibility for whatever injury they may cause upon the manufacturer, who, even if he is not negligent in the manufacture of the product, is responsible for its reaching the market."

Claims for injuries caused by consumer products can be based on several theories:

- manufacturing defect;

- design defect;

- inadequate warning;

- battery (a device was intentionally broken; and

- other theories, depending on what caused the injury.

To win a lawsuit, a plaintiff must demonstrate all four elements applicable to the strict liability in consumer products cases:

1) Defendant must be a merchant who routinely deals with the kinds of goods that are at issue (not a casual or accidental seller).

2) Evidence that a product is defective. There are three kinds of defects:

a) Manufacturing Defect: If a product differs from all other products that came from the same assembly line, making it more dangerous than a consumer would expect;

b) Design Defect: If a product has a design defect if there exists a safer, more practical and cost-effective way to build it, but the merchant has chosen not to implement it for some reason; and

c) Informational Defect (also known as Defect in Marketing): Exists when using a product involves some risk that cannot be avoided, and a consumer was not given adequate warning regarding that risk. If it is possible to make a product safer, a merchant cannot escape liability even when it gives extensive warnings.

3) A product has not been altered since it left defendant's possession. If a product is moved through the ordinary chain of distribution (manufacturer to wholesaler to retailer to customer), it is assumed that it was not altered, and it is up to the defendant to prove otherwise. This presumption is not applicable to the sale of used goods.

4) A plaintiff must use a product in a foreseeable way. A foreseeable use is not limited to the one intended by a manufacturer or a seller. Many misuses are foreseeable, even if they may not be ordinary. For example, people often stand on a chair to change a light bulb; accordingly, it is foreseeable that a chair is not used for sitting only.

Defenses

Plaintiff's comparative fault, gross negligence in using the product or an abnormal unpredictable use, is an affirmative defense in the cases of strict product liability. Other common defenses are:

State-of-the-Art Defense: At the time the product was manufactured or sold, there was no other practical or reasonable alternative design for the product that would have made it less dangerous and still useful for its purpose.

Assumption of Risk: An ordinary person using the product would know it was dangerous and would exercise care in using the product. If he or she did not, he or she thereby agreed to the inherent risk.

Adequate Warnings: Although the product was dangerous, adequate warnings or instructions were included with the product.

Altering or Misusing the Product: The injury resulted from the user altering or misusing the product, unless the misuse could be reasonably foreseen by the manufacturer.

Superseding Cause: A safe product was made unsafe by the occurrence of a superseding event such as a criminal or third-party act, etc.

Statute of Limitation: The general time period for filing products liability lawsuits for personal injuries is two years. For property damages caused by a defective product, it is three years. This time period begins to run on the date of the injury.

A defendant in a product liability action may be able to raise other traditional defenses available in tort cases as well as certain defenses unique to specific product liability actions. The availability of these defenses will vary from state to state.

Damages

There are three general types of damages that may be claimed by a plaintiff in a product liability action: nominal, compensatory, and punitive or exemplary damages.

Although the principal objective of granting damages is compensation for the suffered injuries, in some situations, nominal damages (a trivial sum) may be recovered where a cause of action is proven but no substantial damages are shown. There are two advantages of such an award to a plaintiff: (1) The plaintiff is entitled to costs of a lawsuit; and (2) he or she may be entitled to punitive damages. It is a fundamental principle that a negligent act does not give rise to liability without incurred damages. Hence, where no actual injury has occurred, even nominal damages are not recoverable.

Compensatory damages are designed to actually compensate a plaintiff for the sustained injuries. Recoverable damages include medical bills, economic value of lost earnings over expected lifetime, pain and suffering, a spouse's derivative claim for loss of consortium, and, in some states, other family members' derivative claims for loss of companionship.

In addition to the above damages, punitive damages may be granted if the defendant's conduct has been grossly negligent or outrageous, for the purpose of punishing him or her and deterring the defendant and other market participants from such conduct in the future. Punitive damages may be awarded even though there is no substantial pecuniary or physical harm. A cause of action must be shown in any case, but an award of nominal damages is enough to support further award of punitive damages.

The dramatic increase in the production of varied innovative goods and international trade has led to the constant supply of new or amended products to the U.S. market. The downside is that distributors are increasingly being brought into U.S. courts on allegations of product defects resulting in injuries to American consumers. Merchants should be aware of all laws and regulations applicable to their products so as to prevent any possible violations of law and to be able to react knowledgeably and decisively if called as a party into any legal action.

How to Manage Product Liability Risks

Merchants cannot prevent people from bringing lawsuits against them, but they can improve their chances for a successful defense and expeditious trial by taking certain legal and practical steps.

First, it is important to work on the development of the comprehensive product warnings. The products made available to the general public should incorporate all necessary warnings applicable to both the direct and indirect (foreseeable) use of those products. Extensive warnings help to minimize product liability claims.

Second, merchants should make sure safety measures have been incorporated in the product, including safety instructions, if applicable. For example, products that are dangerous when left unpacked or connected to an electrical outlet should either contain some safety features to prevent injury to users or at least safety instructions, if safety features are not possible or practicable to install. Product safety instructions should be clear, straightforward, and understandable to an average user. If instructions are ambiguous and could be misinterpreted by a layperson, the merchant will be held responsible for any damages or injury that result.

Adequate warnings, safety measures and instructions, standard procedures in manufacturing and distribution of the products, strict compliance with U.S. governmental norms and regulations, and sufficient business insurance are all important parts of business risk management. All possible risks should be carefully considered and evaluated with the assistance of professional consultants before the product enters a U.S. or international market.

CHAPTER 15

Environmental Protection

Environmental law is a complex body of treaties, conventions, statutes, ordinances, and common law that regulates human activities in relation to the natural environment. The U.S. Environmental Protection Agency (EPA) on the federal level and state environmental agencies within their jurisdictions observe and regulate the impact of businesses on the environment. The objectives of the regulations include pollution control, remediation, resource conservation and management. Business owners need to know their obligations under applicable federal and state environmental laws and possible consequences of noncompliance. Compliance requirements differ depending on the type and location of the business.

The main concerns are:

- whether a company is going to operate facilities (real property, equipment, machinery);

- whether a company is going to release or store substances in nature (air, water, land); and

- whether the company will conduct regulated activities for which a government permit is required.

Company owners and managers should work with a legal counsel to identify and address environmental permitting and compliance issues.

Examination of environmental risks should be undertaken before the company actually leases or buys a property, not only in the process of its operation. If environmental agencies find that the property is polluted, both the previous and the present owners will be jointly and severally liable regardless of the time of pollution (meaning, the buyer will be liable even if the property was polluted by the seller or any other third party). Joint and severe liability means each liable person will be held responsible for the total amount of costs to clean up the contamination, even if others are liable as well. If some of the liable people do not have money, the other liable parties must pay full price. The law leaves it to the parties to work out the reimbursement procedure amongst themselves, according to the extent of their involvement.

The federal law, the Comprehensive Environmental Response, Compensation, and Liability Act (CERCLA or Superfund) holds every party liable in an effort to encourage proper investigations and implementation of preventive measures. Under Superfund, the EPA has power to investigate the parties responsible for any release of toxic substance, make them clean up the site at their expense, impose fines and penalties, and even prevent them from continuing their business operations on the site until all procedures are complete. If responsible parties cannot be found or if they do not have adequate financial resources to clean the site, the EPA will clean it up and put a lien against the property. The lien will remain in place until satisfied and transfers to all subsequent owners of the property. For this reason, even before buying or leasing a property it is necessary to conduct environmental investigation to see whether the lien exists or whether some activities took place, which may give rise to the pollution issues.

Comprehensive due diligence is needed not only to ensure that a prospective buyer is not purchasing a property with attached governmental lien, but also to avoid liability of the present owner if the pollution happened with the previous owner but was found out after the transaction took place. Liability under Superfund is strict and exists even when the person handled the hazardous substances carefully or when the person did not even know there was a release. There are only two exceptions to liability. To claim the exception, a company must take certain preventative steps in advance. The first exception to liability for contamination is a bona fide purchaser, who bought the property without knowing it was contaminated. To qualify as a bona fide purchaser, a person must demonstrate that he or she conducted appropriate environmental investigations, made inquiries, and obtained disclosures before the closing. Accordingly, the property was acquired under reasonable reliance on investigation reports and in good-faith belief that the threat of contamination did not exist. The second exception is when contamination of a property was caused solely by an act of the third party such as a neighbor and the owner of the property took precautions against foreseeable acts or omissions by the third parties and against the foreseeable consequences of those acts or omissions, put reasonable measures to prevent the spread of contamination, did not do anything to exacerbate it, and will fully cooperate during the clean-up process (e.g. allowing the clean-up group on the site as needed).

If, during pre-closing investigations, the issue of contamination arises, parties may negotiate and allocate among themselves the percentage of liability and costs in case of the present threat, as well as for any future possibilities of contamination. It is much more advantageous to do it themselves by means of contractual obligations rather than to wait the decision of the court.

After the property is bought or leased, the property owner or operator falls under another set of laws that regulates the operation of the facility. Under Superfund, state, and local laws, the current owners and operators of the facility may be liable for an actual or threatened release of hazardous substances from that facility. The law requires people in charge to implement special practices and procedures directed on the prevention of the hazardous release. The law also prescribes the methods of generation, storage, transportation, and disposition of the hazardous substances on the facilities. It is important to know what are considered hazardous substances in every state where the company operates. Some substances may not be treated as hazardous under Superfund, but may still fall under state law. Federal, state, and local laws supplement each other, and business owners must be familiar and comply with all regulations applicable to their industry.

Another big concern is actual business activities to be conducted, whether they are tied to a particular facility or not. Certain activities require permits issued by the environmental authorities before they can be commenced (e.g. construction, usage or storage of petroleum, release of chemical substances in the air, water, land, etc.). Business owners should identify such activities with their business counsel and obtain all necessary permits beforehand. Most environmental permits are issued by state governments.

If a company is buying existing operations, sometimes (though not always), environmental permits can be transferred to the new owner. The possibility to transfer the necessary permits from the seller to the buyer should be verified well in advance of the business purchase, and the transfer should be concluded at closing. Operating with a permit in the former owner's name can lead to significant liability. If the permits cannot be transferred, a prospective buyer should identify the timeframes and costs of obtaining these permits in his or her name before he or she is able to continue planned business operations.

Once all necessary permits are duly obtained and the regulated activities are commenced, companies also need to be aware of the environmental regulations governing the performance of their activities and those around them. For instance, some laws, in addition to requiring the possession of government-issued permits, also prescribe how a certain activity should be conducted. Companies may have an obligation to report hazardous activities or pollutions that become known to them, even if these are not caused by the companies themselves. The best practice for companies to keep up with the variety of complex regulations is to prepare environmental management manuals and institute implementation programs at the outset of business activities. A good business lawyer can provide guidance to business owners on every step of the process and advise whether the help of other professionals, such as environmental consultants, inspectors, or laboratory workers may be needed.

CHAPTER 16

Regulatory Compliance

Regulatory compliance is generally used to describe the policies and processes companies have in place to ensure that they are following laws, rules, and regulations that are applicable to their industry and jurisdiction. Since there is an extensive variety of federal, state, and local laws and regulations, Congress has created governmental units, bureaus, agencies, departments, commissions, and boards to carry out government regulatory needs, particularly:

- to supervise the compliance of the private sector by requiring periodic reports or establishment of certain practices;

- to provide additional guidance by enacting administrative rules and procedures; and

- to enforce the law by bringing administrative and judicial proceedings.

Governmental agencies can bring investigations, audits, fines, penalties, injunctions, and other administrative and legal actions for noncompliance. The agencies have the authority to hold a public hearing, which is similar to court hearing, and to dispose the matter. If the parties do not agree with the outcome of such a hearing, judicial review is available by request of any involved party.

The goal of the agencies' work is to ensure that private economy is properly functioning, equal opportunities are available to all market participants, no fraudulent or improper practices are utilized by the private companies, interests and rights of the consumers are observed and protected, and that offered products and services are satisfactory both in quality and price. The U.S. regulatory process was established with the goal of setting standards, enforcement, and provision of the services to businesses. Different agencies have authority over a particular industry, and almost all industries are subject to certain compliance requirements. Some of the most popular regulated activities include commerce, import/export, health, agriculture, consumer services, education, welfare, labor, transportation, environment, workplace safety, financial services and transactions, corporate governance, communications, and many others. Accordingly, regular and proper compliance with the applicable laws and regulations is one of a business owner's main concerns.

The overall success and profitability of the business depends on the implementation and compliance with the relevant regulations. Initially, it may seem overwhelming to comply with all applicable regulations, but there are certainly practical, time- and cost-effective ways to deal with it. Business owners should address regulatory issues before establishing a new enterprise and set the necessary procedures of compliance in place during the initial stages of business operations.

The first step should be to identify the federal, state, and local laws and regulations that apply to the company's commercial activities and have the greatest potential to affect its operations and profits.

The second step is, to develop a plan of obtaining all necessary government permits and approvals, based on previous assessments, and to accomplish other required filings within certain time deadlines.

The third step is to develop and implement written policies and mechanisms to regularly verify that the company is in compliance with all requirements. The goal should be to avoid spending too much time and money when performing these obligations on a time-to-time basis. Once a comprehensive regulatory compliance checklist is created, the business owner will have to periodically review it to make sure that all new changes are adopted, but having a predetermined structured compliance plan will save much repeated and overlapping effort for company owners and employees.

The implementation of the comprehensive regulatory compliance mechanisms not only help the management to deal with regulatory matters, but it also demonstrates to the federal and state regulatory officials that the company takes regulatory compliance seriously. When determining how to deal with the companies facing allegations of regulatory non-compliance, enforcement officials are increasingly focused on whether the owners have established internal controls such as the above-mentioned checklist. The internal business policy may influence how much monitoring, oversight, and reporting the company may be subjected to, as well as the extent and nature of potential negative consequences (e.g. fines or injunctions) that a business enterprise and its principals may face.

Governmental agencies can investigate a company on their own initiative if they suspect any sort of noncompliance or if they receive a complaint, including an anonymous one. Some competitors may use the matter of regulatory compliance in bad faith as means of eliminating an active market participant or obtaining some other advantage. To prevent increased regulatory scrutiny, it is even more advantageous to establish a regulatory compliance program in advance and be prepared for any regulatory investigations that may arise. Once all documents are in place, it does not take a lot of time or employment resources to assemble and submit the required proof of compliance. Consequently, agency inquiries do not interrupt the regular course of business activities.

CHAPTER 17

Antitrust Law and Regulations

The United States antitrust law seeks to prohibit anticompetitive behavior and unfair business practices while encouraging competition and development in the marketplace. The competition is deemed a necessary ingredient of a healthy economy, since it benefits both the markets and the consumers. U.S. antitrust law renders illegal certain business practices that may hurt free markets or consumers or both. Various antitrust laws and regulations were adopted on both federal and state levels. While federal laws primarily govern interstate commerce, state laws regulate the conduct of market participants within their state borders. In addition to the enacted laws the Federal Trade Commission (FTC), state antitrust agencies have administrative authority to implement additional regulations, expanding upon existing antitrust laws, to ban new anticompetitive practices that were not in existence at the time when original legal acts were introduced. Anticompetitive laws are also enforced by private litigants who sustain damages as a result of someone practicing prohibited behavior.

The consequences of antitrust law violations can be severe. The company, individual officers, directors, and other businesspeople responsible for such conduct can be subject to both civil and criminal penalties. If intentional and clear violations are proven, criminal penalties may be up to $100 million for a corporation and $1 million for an individual, along with up to 10 years in prison. Additionally, customers, competitors, and others harmed by the conduct may recover damages against the offending party in triplicate of their actual damages, plus attorney fees.

Federal laws and regulations that govern antitrust matters can be quite complex in certain situations since they aim not only to remedy the actual violation, but also to prevent the future ones. Below is an overview of the three core federal antitrust laws:

1. Contracts, Combinations, or Conspiracies in Restraint of Trade

The Sherman Act broadly prohibits "[e]very contract, combination, in the form of trust or otherwise, or conspiracy, in restraint of trade or commerce." Generally speaking, a restraint of trade is an agreement among two or more persons or entities that affects the competitive process. However, the U.S. Supreme Court long ago decided that the Sherman Act does not prohibit every restraint of trade, only unreasonable ones. For instance, an agreement between two individuals to form a partnership restrains competition in some way, but it may not do so unreasonably, and thus may be lawful under the antitrust laws. On the other hand, certain acts are considered so inherently harmful to competition that they are almost always illegal. These acts are called per se violations. Once such actions are detected, the blamed party is not allowed to introduce any defense or justification. Accordingly, when examining the complained conduct, the courts now apply either (1) a per se analysis when the rules are clear, or (2) a broader rule of reason analysis when the rules are not as clear as in cases of per se violations. When applying the rule of reason analysis, in order to evaluate whether conduct was reasonable under circumstances or its sole purpose was to restrain the competition, a fact-intensive inquiry into the motive, purpose, conduct itself, and its effects, including any business justifications, is required.

An illegal antitrust agreement includes implied understandings between the parties, even though they are not written or expressly agreed to. Such agreement may be evident when, after several meetings, companies begin to conduct commercial activities in a certain uniform way that may harm the markets or consumers but benefit those companies. Anticompetitive agreements may exist between different market participants, between those who occupy similar positions in the market as well as those who are on different levels in the market chain.

Agreements Among Competitors: Not all agreements among competitors violate antitrust laws. In the multi-firm sphere, an agreement to cooperate with the purpose of producing better goods and services is not unreasonable, although it technically restrains competition. However, the following types of agreements are determined to be per se violations, which means they automatically violate the antitrust laws and cannot have any justification:

• Agreements to alter, fix, or maintain the prices at which their products and/or services are sold.

• Agreements to allocate customers or divide markets. These violations are not limited to geographic market division; rather, competing firms may not agree not to compete for specific customers or types of customers, products, or territories among themselves.

• Agreements about predatory pricing and biddings. Predatory pricing occurs when companies price their products or services below actual cost, with the purpose of removing competitors from the market (e.g., a product sale price is lower than the actual cost of its production). Predatory bidding occurs when a company bids up the price of raw materials or other inputs to prevent competing companies from acquiring needed materials. Large companies with big budgets may afford to sustain temporary losses in return of taking bigger gains later if they put their smaller competitors out of business; the law prohibits such unethical behavior.

• Agreements about collusive bidding, meaning that two or more competitors agree to alter their bids for the purchase or provision of a particular product or service.

• Agreements among competitors that all of them will refuse to do business with a targeted individual or business or to do business only on certain agreed-upon terms (known as a group boycott agreement).

Agreements with Suppliers and Distributors: The antitrust laws also affect the relationships between the firms at various levels of the supply chain, such as manufacturer/dealer or supplier/manufacturer. Restraints in the supply chain are tested for their reasonableness by analyzing the market in detail and balancing any harmful competitive effects against offsetting benefits. The arrangements in such chains may violate the antitrust laws if they reduce competition among firms at the same level (e.g., if a supplier does not treat all his customers equally, the competition may be reduced among its retailers or wholesalers) or prevent new firms from entering the market (high entrance barrier). Different arrangements between parties are reasonable when, for example, the discount in price is given to one retailer but not to another, based on the buying volume, delivery and production costs, and for other industry-accepted reasons.

A wide variety of agreements may exist between businesses, and these may be anticompetitive, pro-competitive, or competitively neutral. In such case, the conduct at issue must be evaluated under the rule of reason analysis, considering and balancing possible harms and benefits. If a court determines that the competitive harms of the agreement outweigh its benefits, it is deemed an illegal restraint of trade. As a sample, some types of the illegal agreements that may exist between the various participants in the supply chain are provided below:

• Price discrimination, when a supplier charges competing purchasers different prices for the same goods (this does not apply to services) or discriminates in the provision of allowances, compensation for advertising, provision of additional free goods for samples and other services. Price discrimination may give favored customers an edge in the market that has nothing to do with their superior efficiency. In general, the law requires that a seller treat all competing customers in a proportionately fair and equitable manner. If the seller offers additional services or goods, such as the use of its facilities, advertisement, and promotional materials, it must inform all of its competing customers about the availability of such services or allowances. Price discrimination is lawful if it reflects the different costs of dealing with different buyers or is the result of the seller's attempts to meet a competitor's offering. Discrimination in allowances is generally forbidden. Again, when evaluating a particular situation, the rule of reason is applied.

• Exclusive dealings involve an agreement between the parties to purchase the goods/services exclusively from each other. In practice, such contracts are common and permissible, but they should be reasonable. For example, the manufacturer may give lower price to its exclusive dealers.

• Territorial and customer restrictions are also not allowed. A manufacturer or supplier may assign a specific territory to a distributor, but it may not prohibit a distributor from selling its products outside the assigned territory without justification.

• Pricing impositions are forbidden. A manufacturer or supplier may not establish prices at which its distributors resell its products. However, manufacturers are free to suggest resale prices and even unilaterally refuse to do business with a distributor who fails to comply with these suggested prices.

• Tying arrangements are agreements in which one party agrees to do business with another party only on condition that the other party does something else in addition to the primary agreement. For example, a seller will only agree to sell widgets to a buyer on the condition that the buyer will also either (1) purchase knickknacks from the seller or (2) guarantee that it will not buy knickknacks from another seller. Tying arrangement is a per se violation.

2. Single-Firm Conduct

In an effort to gain market share, companies sometimes employ forms of conduct or tactics that go beyond competition on the merits and that may harm or distort normal competition. Competitive conduct may be justifiable if it is innovative and actually benefits consumers. However, if there is no valid reason for that conduct other than to reduce or eliminate competition and charge higher prices, it will be precisely prohibited by antitrust laws.

The Sherman Act addresses single-firm conduct by providing a remedy against "[e]very person who shall monopolize or attempt to monopolize…any part of the trade or commerce." Monopoly, per se, is not illegal, but only monopoly acquired or maintained through prohibited conduct is forbidden. The company has total rights to try to achieve a monopoly position, even utilizing some aggressive methods. Also, some companies may succeed in the marketplace to the point where they move far beyond their competitors. It was noted in one court decision: "[t]he successful competitor, having been urged to compete, must not be turned on when he wins." Thus, U.S. antitrust law does not attack monopoly power obtained through superior skill, foresight, and industry. The law is violated only if the company tries to maintain or acquire a monopoly through unreasonable and unethical methods. A key factor used by the courts to determine whether or not conduct is unreasonable is whether the practice has a legitimate business justification.

As opposed to the illegal agreements among various market participants, offensive monopoly and attempted monopolization may be committed by an individual firm without the involvement of others. Unreasonable exclusionary practices, predatory pricing, and other methods used by the firm to entrench or create monopoly power can be unlawful.

3. Anticompetitive Mergers and Acquisitions

Many mergers benefit competition and consumers by allowing companies to operate more efficiently, but some change market dynamics in ways that can lead to higher prices, fewer or lower-quality goods or services, and less innovation. To avoid such consequences, the merger review process was established. Federal law prohibits mergers and acquisitions that bear the effect of substantially lessening competition or tend to create a monopoly.

The Hart-Scott-Rodino Act, a federal statute, requires companies intending to merge to file certain information with the Federal Trade Commission (the FTC). This Act allows the FTC to examine the likely effects of the proposed mergers before they take place. This process of advanced review is necessary in order to prevent the undesired mergers from happening rather than dealing with the consequences later. The agency may also investigate the completed mergers if they harm the customers as a result.

In contrast to federal law, there are no filing requirements or specific timing provisions under most state laws. As a result, state antitrust agencies may investigate any merger at any time and may challenge a merger transaction even after it has been consummated without creating any evident harm.

Statistics show that 95 percent of proposed mergers presented to the FTC for review do not have any competitive issues. If a deal presents some problems, it is often possible to resolve those concerns by consent agreement between the parties, which allows the beneficial aspects of the deal to go forward while eliminating the competitive threat. If the agency and the parties cannot agree on a solution, the Commission may seek a court order preventing businesses from merging.

The announcement of a merger can be a headline-grabbing event, especially in cases of large public companies or when the transaction has been valued at a substantial amount. By law, all information provided to or obtained by the governmental agencies in a merger review or investigation process is confidential. Agencies cannot disclose any information regarding the proposed deal, including the existence of a review or investigation. In some situations, however, the parties themselves may announce their merger plans, and the FTC may confirm the ongoing review.

Exemptions to Antitrust Laws

There are several exemptions to antitrust law enforcement, as follows:

Patent Owners: Because public policy favors innovation, patent owners are exempt. However, the use of a fraudulently obtained patent to create or maintain a monopoly subjects the individuals and companies to criminal and civil prosecution.

Labor Unions and Agricultural Organizations: The Clayton Act provides an exemption for labor unions and agricultural organizations.

Banks: The Securities and Exchange Act of 1934 regulates banking entities. The U.S. Supreme Court decided that in cases where securities laws and antitrust laws conflict, securities laws prevail**Nonprofits:** The Nonprofit Institutions Act permits nonprofits to purchase and vendors to supply the products and services for use by such organizations at a reduced price without violating the antitrust laws.

Sports Leagues: Generally, mergers and joint agreements of professional football, baseball, basketball, or hockey leagues are exempt from antitrust law under 15 U.S.C. § 1291 et seq.

Newspapers Under Joint Operating Agreements: These allowed limited antitrust immunity under the Newspaper Preservation Act of 1970.

Insurance Companies: Limited antitrust exemptions are provided by the McCarran-Ferguson Act, 15 U.S.C. § 1011, et seq.

The government may grant monopolies in certain industries, such as utilities and infrastructure, where multiple players are seen as unfeasible or impractical.

Antitrust laws also do not prevent companies from using the legal system or political process to attempt to reduce competition. Most of these activities are considered legal.

Free and open markets are the foundation of a vibrant economy. Aggressive competition among sellers in an open marketplace gives consumers—both individuals and businesses—the benefits of lower prices, higher quality products and services, more choices, and greater innovation. The goal of antitrust laws is to enforce the rules of the competitive marketplace and maintain healthy national economy.

CHAPTER 18

Litigation and Dispute Resolution

Being a business owner has ups and downs. While enjoying independence and hopefully a good profit margin, disputes may occur between companies or between a company and its customers. If parties cannot resolve their disputes via good-faith negotiations, there are several methods of dispute resolution in the United States that involve third parties. The most widely known and obvious is litigation in the U.S. courts. The general process of the lawsuit is outlined below:

1. Plaintiff files complaint with the court and serves defendant with a copy.

2. Defendant answers the complaint or makes a motion in lieu of answer. Defendant may also assert claims against plaintiff if those claims arise from the same circumstances (e.g. the same contract is involved). These are called counterclaims.

3. Discovery begins, the period when all involved parties obtain information and evidence from the other parties. This is accomplished through written demands, depositions of the parties and witnesses, and other legal means. The law does not allow any surprises at trial, meaning that a party cannot introduce new evidence or information to the judge if advance notice was not given to all participants in the lawsuit. During the discovery period and before trial, parties can file various motions asking for court orders. Also, this is the time when preliminary, status, settlement, and other conferences are held between the parties and the judge.

4. If parties cannot reach a settlement agreement after exchanging all evidence and evaluating their chances, the case goes to trial.

5. The decision of the trial court may be appealed to the higher court. If no appeal is made, the final judgment is entered. Depending on its directives, the winning party can commence enforcement procedures.

Commercial lawsuits in U.S. courts are typically expensive and time consuming. Luckily it is not the only option for the aggrieved party. There are alternative dispute resolution methods (ADR) such as arbitration, mediation, or mixed dispute resolution process that allow parties to settle their disputes without involvement of the public court system. These methods are often more cost- and time-effective and give parties more control over the resolution process. Parties may agree in advance, at the initial stage of contract execution, that in case a dispute arises between them, they will try to resolve it by a certain ADR mechanism. The decision of the arbitrator, mediator, or other third-party adviser may be enforced by the courts, but only if the parties agreed to it in advance and properly drafted the relevant contract clause. Parties can also agree to try some methods of ADR before they go to court, but its outcome will not be binding. This is done when parties want to state their positions, evaluate their arguments, and try to settle the dispute before diving into the litigation process.

Mediation: This method is designed to help parties to settle their disputes. A mediator does not decide the case, but instead seeks common grounds among conflicting interests in order to assist the parties in reaching agreement or creating conditions where each party can be a winner. If parties reach an acceptable compromise and both agree, the outcome of the mediation can be binding and filed with the court. Even if no agreement is reached, it is often useful to mediate the matter before going to court. Even during court proceedings, most courts require parties to go through preliminary mediation, hoping to save public and private resources.

Arbitration: This is similar to court proceedings, only no judge or jury is involved. The arbitrator is a neutral party, generally a lawyer or an expert in the subject of the dispute. Arbitration is more structured than mediation. The parties may make oral arguments, submit written statements, call witnesses, and submit evidence. According to the parties' preliminary agreement, the decision of the arbitrator may be binding and entered with the court or unbinding and serve to promote case settlement without trial.

Mixed Dispute Resolution Processes: These include elements of mediation, arbitration, and trials. This process can be sponsored by the court. The parties have opportunity to present their case before the jury prior to engaging in the full-scale trial (summary jury trials). Such proceedings are not binding and serve to give parties a real sense of the possible outcome of the trial. Private processes without court involvement include the use of mini-trials and a combination of arbitration and mediation. Private mini-trials are used when the process of negotiations is not moving forward. Parties choose a neutral adviser who will hear the case and ask the parties privately about the strengths and weaknesses of their case. Then the adviser can render his or her opinion regarding how the parties should proceed. The opinion of the adviser and the outcome of the private mini-trials are not binding and serve only as evaluation and facilitation mechanism. The mixture of arbitration and mediation is a process where parties mediate their dispute before submitting it to the binding arbitration. If the parties cannot reach an agreement during mediation, the case will be decided by the arbitrator, whose decision will be binding. Still this process can be a time- and money-saving method for both parties, as compared to the painstaking process of litigation.

ADR is a good alternative to litigation in many commercial transactions. Nevertheless, it may not be the optimal method in every business situation. Parties should carefully discuss with their attorneys whether it is beneficial to include arbitration, mediation, or another alternative dispute resolution clause in a particular contract. There are certain situations when court involvement may be necessary. For example, if one party may need to prevent the other party from doing something in the future rather than just curing a past breach, the court can react quickly by issuing a temporary restraining order. Arbitrators might have the power to issue similar orders, but they are often not in the position to react quickly enough. One such example is when an intellectual property license agreement is breached. Such agreements are not only about the payment of money, but the licensor is concerned that the licensee will not act beyond the scope of the license or disclose some trade secrets to the third parties. If a party is not expeditiously served with a restraining order, whether the other party prevails or not in the final dispute resolution, the consequences may be irreversible. To combine quick mechanisms of the courts and inexpensive procedures of ADR, it is possible to state in the contract that disputes and claims between the parties will be resolved by arbitration (or other ADR method), but the parties reserve the right to seek interlocutory relief from a court (temporary orders before the final resolution of the matter, as mentioned above).

Dispute resolution processes can be time consuming, complex, and expensive. But they are more manageable than is often believed. The foreseeability and manageability of the possible disputes are essential part of doing business. It is important to understand the U.S. litigation process and available alternative dispute resolution methods in order to make the right decision and to avoid unpredictability.

CHAPTER 19

Business and Employment Immigration to the United States

We live in the age of globalization. By no means professionals are constrained by their physical locations. Very often, people can offer the benefits of their business ventures or professional services to a much wider range of customers than domestic markets. Companies grow, generating higher profits and creating additional jobs. Consequently, the need to open subsidiaries and hire additional workforce emerges.

The U.S. market is one of the most lucrative in the world, both because of the growth opportunities it offers to the companies and because of the buying power of its consumers. Many foreign companies, entrepreneurs, and professionals are looking to the United States as a dream place to establish their business presence.

U.S. immigration laws are very favorable to people who are eager and ready to use their resources, knowledge, skills, and abilities for the development of the country's economy. The laws allow foreign companies to open subsidiaries in the U.S. and relocate their own personnel here for work. U.S.-based companies are also free to utilize professional services of foreign nationals and can bring those nationals to the U.S. under a number of different immigration categories.

Companies who seek to bring foreign employees to the United States most commonly use the following visa categories: B-1 (a visa waiver program for some qualified individuals), H1-B, E, O, P, TN, and L. After initially obtaining a temporary non-immigrant visa in one of these categories, if a foreign national has the right combination of skills, education, work experience and is otherwise eligible, later he or she may be able to obtain permanent resident status (a Green Card) in the United States. Every year, U.S. Citizenship and Immigration Services issues approximately 140,000 immigrant visas to aliens, their spouses, and children who seek to immigrate to the United States based on their professional skills.

Let's review the basic requirements for these various visas:

B-1 Visa: This is a business visitor's visa that enables a business traveler to visit and stay in the United States for a short period of time, usually up to six months, with possibility to extend that stay for the same consecutive periods of time. It does not grant employment authorization in the United States, meaning that the foreign national cannot receive salary and look for a job in the U.S. The purpose of this visa is to allow foreign businesspeople and their employees to come to the U.S. temporarily in order to promote their business, gauge the market, solicit sales from U.S. customers and businesses, negotiate contracts, and attend business meetings and conferences.

Visa Waiver Program: This is a substitution for the B-1 visa for the citizens of most European countries, Japan, and certain other countries that may be qualified to enter the United States for a period of ninety days without applying and receiving a B-1 visa. The requirements to the business travelers under Visa Waiver Program are the same as to the B-1 holders. They cannot receive compensation or seek employment in the United States. Foreign nationals entering the United States under the Visa Waiver Program qualifications must depart by the expiration of this ninety-day period, and no extensions of stay are granted.

H1-B Visa: This visa is available to individuals coming to the United States to be employed by a U.S.-based company in a specialty occupation or profession. Specialty occupations include those that require the services of a professional with either a university degree or special skills obtained through training and work experience. H-1B visas are issued for an initial period of three years and may be extended for additional three years, for a maximum consecutive period of six years. The holders of H-1B visas may be eligible to apply for a permanent residence in the United States, provided their employers attest that they need the services of those aliens for a longer period than just a few years. It is important to note that a sponsored employee will continue to be an employee at will, meaning that an employer can fire him or her anytime, at the employer's sole discretion. The termination of employment may influence the employee's immigration process, but the immigration procedures cannot restrict the employer in its right to hire or fire the employee.

Employers sponsoring H-1B aliens for immigration must obtain approval from the U.S. Department of Labor, certifying that the employment of that particular foreign national will not adversely affect the U.S. labor market and that the employer is financially capable to pay the prevailing wage to that foreign employee. The labor certification procedure may be waived if the foreign national can establish that he or she will be doing something significant and useful to U.S. national interests. For example, an entrepreneur might be able to demonstrate that his or her business enterprise will create jobs for U.S. workers or otherwise enhance the welfare of the United States. Physical therapists, professional nurses, and persons of extraordinary ability are exempt from the labor certificate procedure as well because they possess professional skills that are useful and needed in the country.

E Visa: The United States has treaties with many foreign countries providing that, in order to promote international trade, if a U.S. company conducts substantial trade with a particular foreign country, it can employ and bring to the United States the executives, managers, and other individuals who hold essential skills from that foreign country under the E-1 visa category. A trade is considered substantial when there are regular numerous transactions over a period of time, as opposed to several random transactions, and the income derived is enough to support the treaty trader.

If a foreign company or individual invests or is in the process of actively investing substantial capital in the U.S. enterprise, they are considered treaty investors and can come to the United States themselves or bring their employees to direct the operations of that enterprise. A substantial amount of capital is not measured by numbers; rather, it is an amount that meets the following three criteria:

- It is substantial in relationship to the total cost of either purchasing an established enterprise or creating the type of a new enterprise that are being considered;

- it is sufficient to ensure the treaty investor's financial commitment to the enterprise's success; and

• it is objectively enough to support the likelihood that the treaty investor will successfully develop and direct the enterprise.

E visas are generally issued in increments of up to five years. They can be reissued indefinitely, as long as the investment or trade and nationality requirements for eligibility continue to be met. The holders of E visas are eligible to apply for a permanent residence in the United States. E-1 and E-2 holders (if they received this status as employees of a company investor, not as individual investors themselves) are required to be sponsored by their employers similar to H1-B visa holders.

There is an EB-2 immigrant category for foreign investors that allows for self-sponsorship. This category is reserved for individuals, who wish to reside permanently in the United States with the intent of creating or developing a business enterprise in the U.S. The required amount of investment per each individual investor is $1 million or $500,000 (if the investment is made in a targeted employment area) in a new commercial enterprise that employs at least 10 full-time U.S. workers or in an existing commercial enterprise that requires said investment for further development and creation of 10 additional employment positions for U.S. workers.

O-1 Visa: This is available to aliens with exceptional ability in science, arts, education, athletics, or business. To obtain O-1 classification, an alien must establish that he or she has achieved national or international acclaim. An O-1 petition may be approved for an initial period of three years, and extensions may be granted in one-year increments. Aliens with exceptional ability usually need employment sponsorship for immigration purposes. Aliens with extraordinary ability, however, do not need an employment sponsorship and can be self-sponsored, as mentioned above in the discussion of labor certification requirements for certain professional immigrants. An alien of *extraordinary* ability must demonstrate that he or she has risen to the very top among all other members of his or her professional field and that his or her achievements have been recognized and sustained national or international acclaim. The alien of *exceptional* ability, on the other hand, must only demonstrate that his or her professional qualities are above those possessed by an average professional in his or her field, but those qualities do not necessarily have to place the alien among the very few individuals at the top of the relative profession.

P Visa: The P visa is available for internationally recognized athletes or entertainers. It allows artists and athletes to come to the United States temporarily to perform in their professional capacity, individually or as part of a group, under a reciprocal exchange program between an organization in the United States and an organization in another country. The difference between a P visa and an O visa is that to obtain a P visa the foreign nationals do not have to demonstrate the possession of any exceptional ability; they only have to show that they are members of the above professions and are coming to the U.S. with the purpose of participating in a certain cultural exchange program. P visa itself cannot serve as a basis for immigration, but a foreign national can apply for a permanent status under any other category if he or she can satisfy the particular requirements of that category.

TN or NAFTA Visa: This permits citizens of Canada and Mexico to work in the United States in certain specialty occupations that are listed in the North American Free Trade Agreement (NAFTA) Sec. 214 (e)(2). Some examples are lawyers, accountants, and engineers. TN visas are granted for three years for the initial period of stay and may be extended in three-year increments indefinitely. This type of visa allows Canadian and Mexican professionals to enter and stay in the United States with the purpose of practicing in their field without first obtaining employment in the country, as is usually required for all other nationals.

L-1 Visa: This is an intracompany transferee visa and enables a foreign company to transfer its employees from one of its foreign offices to its office in the United States if such office already exists or to send an employee to the U.S. to establish a new office for the company. This visa category is available for managers, executives, and individuals with specialized knowledge of the foreign company's business or products, those who have worked for that foreign company at least one year within the preceding three years.Many foreign business owners would prefer to be physically present themselves in U.S. territory or to transfer their skilled employees to the U.S. branch of their company in order to successfully operate a business venture here rather than hiring local managers. The national policy of the U.S. government is very welcoming to foreign entrepreneurs. They boost the U.S. economy directly by bringing foreign capital, creating new businesses, new employment positions, and paying taxes in the United States, and indirectly by contributing to the overall development of the U.S. market. As a matter of fact, the U.S. government has created multiple incentives for foreign business owners to run their businesses in the United States, and favorable immigration policy is one of them.

L visas are issued for an initial period of one or three years and can be extended thereafter for up to seven years. L visa holders can travel outside the United States unrestricted, so there is no requirement that a person continuously stays in the country during the visa term. Holders of L-1 visas are entitled to apply for a permanent residence status after a year of their presence in the country.

As mentioned above, L-1 visas can be issued to two categories of foreign workers: 1) to aliens coming to the United States to perform services in a <u>managerial capacity</u> and 2) to those coming to perform services that require <u>specialized knowledge</u> related to that particular company. A person is considered to be in a managerial capacity, when he or she is authorized to make managerial decisions on behalf of the company. If a business owner is willing to come to the United States him- or herself, he or she will indisputably come here in a managerial capacity. A person is considered to posses a specialized knowledge if he or she knows the specifications of the foreign company's product, service, research, equipment, techniques, management, or other interests or has an advanced level of knowledge or expertise in the employing organization's processes and procedures. This visa does not cover absolutely all, even non-essential, foreign employees, such as supporting staff. The reason is that easily substituted workers may be freely hired in the United States, and there is no need for a foreign company to bring them from oversees.

Certain requirements must be met by employees and the company itself before they can apply for a L visa:

- An alien must have worked for the sending company for at least one year within the last three-year period. This one year of employment does not necessarily have to be the year preceding visa application, but any one-year period during the preceding three years.

- A company must demonstrate that it has the financial capability to remunerate the alien and to begin doing business in the United States. There is no requirement as to the amount of capital, but it should be enough to support the foreigner in the U.S. for a period of one year.

If, after a year of doing business in the United States, the alien wishes to request permanent residence (a Green Card), his or her company can petition U.S. Immigration Services on that employee's behalf. To be an eligible sponsor, the company must show that it has been conducting regular business activities on U.S. soil during the preceding year. Again, there are no requirements as to the amount of revenue or the financial state of the company. In order to demonstrate that the U.S. subsidiary has actually been conducting business, and is not just a passive representative office of the foreign company in the United States, the company must provide evidence of regular, systematic, and continuous business affairs. Examples include provision of goods and/or services to its customers, research or creation of new product/service or otherwise doing whatever is relevant to the particular industry. Since there are no capital requirements, L visas are available to businesses of any size.

Employment and business immigration laws provide great opportunity for foreign entrepreneurs and professionals to come to the United States for a long period of time or to immigrate here permanently. As long as a person is willing to contribute his or her valuable services and expertise to the U.S. market, the country makes various options available. It is no wonder the U.S. economy is one of the largest and most dynamic in the world.

CONCLUSION

This book has provided you with an overview of U.S. business law, the rights and interests of the market participants, the consequences of ignorance or noncompliance, and how the courts and other government agencies determine liability of the parties. We've also explored possible practical solutions and strategies to ensure that your business is operating on the right footing.

Looking ahead, we can see that nowadays business industries develop pretty quickly. Business law must accommodate and accompany this new reality. With the development of the Internet and new technologies, new statutes and regulations are adopted and existing ones must sometimes be adapted. It is good that current legal principles are flexible enough and can be applied consistently, but it is the prime responsibly of the market participants to know and follow them.

Business development and growth is a constant process. The events during this journey will require implementation of new skills and information. Having the right resources ensures the availability of choice and flexibility. An accurate understanding of rights and responsibilities allows entrepreneurs to have more control and competence and be better prepared for the changing or challenging times. Knowing the playing field of the business reality sets businesspeople up for more expeditious success and a brighter future. It is our human right to be bolder, better, stronger, happier, and fulfilled. Every market participant should know how to protect his or her assets that allow the business venture to grow.

My intention is that you refer to this book multiple times, whenever a particular need emerges in your professional life. You will discover greater clarity about the business world and the interactions between its participants, a deeper understanding of the business principles, and more profound anticipation of the business events. You do not have to operate blindly, contemplating doubts, insecurities, and dilemmas. You now realize how much informational resources matter in all business endeavors, giving entrepreneurs a clear, pure picture about their positions and those of the people around them.

My genuine hope is that this book will be a helpful companion to you during your fertile and rewarding working years. The world is rich with opportunities to express your unique skills and qualities. Give yourself permission to activate your best efforts and character, pursue your most distant goals, commit and achieve something meaningful, enjoy your great accomplishments, and widely celebrate your success! It is time to live your dreams!

APPENDIX

References and Links to Useful Resources

U.S. Small Business Administration, www.sba.gov

U.S. Chamber of Commerce, www.uschamber.com

Internal Revenue Service, www.irs.gov

U.S. Census Bureau, www.census.gov

Central Intelligence Agency, www.cia.gov/library/publications/the-world-factbook/geos/us.html8

U.S. Securities and Exchange Commission, www.sec.gov

New York Stock Exchange, nyse.nyx.com

NASDAQ Stock Market, www.nasdaq.com

U.S. Department of Labor, www.dol.gov

U.S. Department of State, www.state.gov

U.S. Bureau of Labor Statistics, www.bls.gov

Federal Occupational Safety and Health Administration, www.osha.gov/as/opa/oshafaq.html

Social Security Administration, www.ssa.gov

U.S. Citizenship and Immigration Service, www.uscis.gov

Objective measures of business regulations, climate, cost and ranking in 183 countries, www.doingbusiness.org

Small Business Taxes and Management, www.smbiz.com

U.S. Department of Education, www.ed.gov

Resources on Starting and Managing a Business, www.usa.gov/Business/Business-Gateway.shtml

Federal Trade Commission, www.ftc.gov

Bureau of Consumer Protection, Business Center, business.ftc.gov

American Institute of Certified Public Accountants, www.aicpa.org/Pages/Default.aspx

State Governments and State Agencies Directories, www.statelocalgov.net

U.S. Department of Transportation, www.dot.gov

U.S. Commercial Service (helping U.S. companies export), export.gov

U.S. Patent and Trademark Office, www.state.gov

U.S. Copyright Office, copyright.gov

U.S. Customs and Border Protection, www.cbp.gov

U.S. International Trade Commission, usitc.gov

U.S. Food and Drug Administration, www.fda.gov

U.S. Federal Reserve System, www.federalreserve.gov

U.S. Department of Justice, www.justice.gov

U.S. Environmental Protection Agency, www.epa.gov

Crowdfunding Sites: www.indiegogo.com; www.kickstarter.com; wefunder.com; www.startupaddict.com; startsomegood.com; www.rockethub.com; www.pozible.com; www.quirky.com; www.causes.com; newjelly.com; mycofolio.com; peerbackers.com

Online Funding Platforms: www.go4funding.com; thefunded.com; www.ycombinator.com; www.fundinguniverse.com; www.gobignetwork.com; www.vfinance.com

Funding Sources for Female-Owned Businesses: www.goldenseeds.com; www.phenomenelleangels.com; www.womensvcfund.com; www.springboardenterprises.org; www.illuminate.com; www.ceresventurefund.com; www.sba.gov/content/contracting-opportunities-women-owned-small-businesses; www.wvf-ny.org; www.opportunityfund.org

Money Matters: bills.com (to calculate all your bills); annualcreditreport.com (free credit reports); portfolio.moningstar.com (portfolio returns tracker); Mint.com; Moneycenter.yodlee.com; QuickenOnline.com (to see all your money at a single glance)

Useful Business Publications: www.startupnation.com/knowledge-hub; www.inc.com; money.cnn.com; www.sbtv.com; www.forbes.com

Inspirational Resources: anthonyrobbins.com; drdemartini.com; www.wisebrain.org; www.authentichappiness.sas.upenn.edu/Default.aspx; dreamuniversity.com; www.businessballs.com/index.htm; www.nlpco.com

Printed in the United States of America

61624714R00115

Made in the USA
Middletown, DE
12 January 2018